Key Contemporary Thinkers

Published

Peter Burke, *The Annales School*
Simon Evnine, *Donald Davidson*
Christopher Hookway, *Quine: Language, Experience and Reality*
Douglas Kellner, *Jean Baudrillard: From Marxism to Post-Modernism and Beyond*
Georgia Warnke, *Gadamer: Hermeneutics, Tradition and Reason*

Forthcoming

Michael Best, *Galbraith*
Michael Caesar, *Umberto Eco*
Homi Bhabha, *Edward Said and Orientalism*
Jocelyn Dunphy, *Paul Ricoeur*
David Frisby, *Walter Benjamin: An Introduction to His Social Theory*
Andrew Gamble, *Hayek and the Market Order*
John Hall, *Raymond Aron: A Study in French Intellectual Culture*
Phillip Hansen, *Hannah Arendt*
Adrian Hayes, *Talcott Parsons and the Theory of Action*
Eileen Manion, *Mary Daly: Religion and Radical Feminism*
Phil Manning, *Erving Goffman and Modern Sociology*
Makiko Minow-Pinkey, *Kristeva*
Michael Moriarty, *Roland Barthes*
Hans-Peter Muller, *Culture, Power and Class: The Social Theory of Pierre Bourdieu*
William Outhwaite, *Habermas*
Simon Schaffer, *Kuhn*
Geoff Stokes, *Popper*
Jonathan Wolff, *Nozick*
Ian Whitehouse, *Rorty*

RAWLS

A Theory of Justice and its Critics

Chandran Kukathas and Philip Pettit

Polity Press

First published 1990 by Polity Press
in association with Basil Blackwell

Editorial office:
Polity Press, 65 Bridge Street,
Cambridge CB2 1UR, UK

Marketing and production:
Basil Blackwell Ltd
108 Cowley Road, Oxford OX4 1JF, UK

ISBN 0 7456 0281 9
ISBN 0 7456 0282 7 (pbk)

British Library Cataloguing in Publication Data
A CIP catalogue record for this book is available from the British Library.

Typeset in 11 on 13 pt Times by
Wearside Tradespools, Fulwell, Sunderland
Printed in Great Britain by Billings & Sons, Worcester

For Nathan, Rory, Owen, Samuel and Sarah

Contents

Foreword

This book will be picked up, so our publishers assure us, by readers across a wide spectrum; at one extreme, those who come fresh to the reading of Rawls; at the other, those who come well seasoned. The book is designed to provide some sense of Rawls's theory, and of its significance in contemporary political philosophy, for those who come fresh. But we hope that it also has something to offer seasoned readers.

The first chapter sets the background against which Rawls's book *A Theory of Justice* made such an impact. It is mainly a piece of historical interpretation but it also offers a discussion of the moral individualism that characterizes the tradition to which the book belongs. The second chapter focuses on the contractarian character of Rawls's theory, offering an account of his method plus an analysis and taxonomy of contractarian approaches in general. The third chapter presents Rawls's substantive claims about justice and his detailed arguments for them. It leads into the fourth chapter where we argue that Rawls rests his case much more heavily than is usually recognized on considerations of feasibility than on considerations as to what the parties to his contract would find desirable.

The last three chapters are equally designed to keep the interest of the seasoned reader, while remaining accessible to beginners. Chapter 5 describes and assesses the libertarian critique of Rawls's theory, in particular that provided by Robert Nozick. Chapter 6 does the same service or disservice for the rather more amorphous communitarian critique, associated with writers like Alasdair MacIntyre, Michael Sandel, Charles Taylor and Michael Walzer. Finally, the last chapter looks at Rawls's emerging self-interpretation and self-critique, distinguishing two phases of development, one more Kantian, the other more Hegelian.

The book might well have contained a further chapter, looking at more detailed criticisms of Rawls's approach. *A Theory of Justice* has been the stimulus, not just for grand critique in the libertarian or communitarian style, but also for fine-grained explorations that look at the priority of liberty in Rawls, the role of the notion of equality, the precise significance of the difference principle, and such matters. This literature is at the centre of contemporary analytical discussions and it is often of a very high calibre. We have decided not to include a chapter on such material, not because we do not think it would be interesting, but rather because our judgment is that the job could not be adequately done in a short compass. (See Daniels 1978; Pogge 1989.)

It is necessary for any political theorist today to take stock of Rawls and of the debates he has stimulated. We have used the invitation to write this book as an opportunity to do some of our own stock-taking. We do not offer a final, rounded assessment of Rawls and his critics but we try to indicate our own views as we go along. For the record, the sort of picture we project is this: that Rawls's theory of justice is of outstanding importance, showing the way for a revival of political theory; that while it is contractarian in character, it does not by any means exhaust the resources of contractarian thinking; that though it is contractarian in character, it rests in good part on considerations of feasibility which are accessible to all approaches; that the libertarian critique is not so much a critique as the statement of an alternative perspective on the political world; that the communitarian critique is in many ways overstated, failing to allow for all the moves at Rawls's disposal, or indeed for all the moves he actually makes; and that Rawls's self-interpretation and self-critique is uncertain in direction and, most recently, has taken an unfortunate turn, with the hardening of his aspirations for a political philosophy to end all political philosophies.

This much, representing the general lines of argument in the book, we certainly share. But as is inevitable, particularly given that we favour different political philosophies, our views may sometimes come apart in detail. Before the court of final judgement Pettit is primarily responsible for chapters 1, 2 and 5, Kukathas for chapters 3, 6 and 7; the jury is still out on chapter 4. We have tried to knit our claims and discussions closely together. Were it not for our becoming honesty, we like to think that readers might not have noticed the seams.

For their help in preparing the manuscript for publication we would like to give special thanks to Shirley Ramsay of the Department of Politics at the Australian Defence Force Academy and Anne Robinson of the Research School of Social Sciences at the Australian National University. We are also particularly grateful to Brian Beddie for helpful comments on chapter 7, and to Andrew Williams and the two anonymous referees who read and commented extensively on an earlier draft of the book.

A Ne

'No commanding v
20th century.' So
outstanding differ
is no longer true.
of Justice by Jo
Cambridge, Mas
James Fishkin a

Political theory
thinking about
1960, 37). It rai
there be a stat
ought it to be
citizens? But s
us as long at
John Rawls h
work in 1971
chapter.

By way of
of political

necessary to
theory, tradi
what is politi
desirable on

Suppose we
alleviate prob
and the questi
There are tw
seeking an ans

The first av
describe them,
things our gr
poverty, so th
should take se
cannot hope to
rough and only
hood. We may
anything useful
for a drop-out
attention on wh
who reside perm

The other ave
into issues of d
want to know t
attempt in helpin
financial help a
provide help in
shelter for the n
outs, attempting
various kinds?

The exploration
ably characterizes
tasks which some
lesson extends to t
state and governm
find that political
simultaneously wi
government and its

This distinction between feasibility and desirability studies helps us to see what happened in the twentieth century which explains Berlin's harsh judgement on the state of things in 1962. There are three points to make.

The first is that in the course of this century, with the progressive demarcation and professionalization of disciplines like economics, political science and philosophy, the two sides of political theory tended to come more and more apart. Economic and political scientists prided themselves on their self-description as scientists and, in line with presumptions then current, took this to mean that they could not involve themselves with matters of desirability; their domain was one of facts, not of values. On the other side philosophers, with the exception of some Marxists, were anxious to maintain the claim of their discipline to be analytic or *a priori* – this applied on the Continent as well as elsewhere – and took the view that philosophy could have nothing to say on questions of feasibility; an *a priori* discipline can only rely on abstract or logical analysis to answer its questions, and matters of feasibility seemed to require empirical investigation. This division of disciplines meant therefore that there was no single group of professionals who could claim to pursue simultaneously the feasibility and desirability studies required for political theory.

So much for the separation of those studies. The second and third points we wish to make bear respectively on the fate of these pursuits in isolation from one another.

The exploration of the desirable ends of the state might seem to be a job which philosophy could have reasonably pursued, even in isolation from questions of feasibility. But the task was generally neglected in favour of a higher-order activity: the analysis of the concepts relevant to the judgement of desirability or, in Continental mode, the analysis of our experiences of value or desirability. Thus the annals of early twentieth-century philosophy are long on rival analyses of utility and liberty and equality but extremely short on arguments in favour of these or other ideals. This retreat from advocacy to commentary is probably explicable by the fact that, given the widespread presumption that science deals with facts only, philosophers were loath to present themselves as defenders of any particular values. There may have seemed to be little room for providing an intellectually respectable defence of any values, at least in the absence of feasibility constraints.

The isolated exploration of the feasible did not fare much better than the isolated exploration of the desirable. Feasibility studies are only interesting in relation to specific desirability proposals and, given the vaunted value-freedom of economics and political science, it is not surprising that in the twentieth century those disciplines did little to advance feasibility studies. Welfare economics is primarily a feasibility discipline but it became focused only on the feasibility of maximizing utility via market institutions and later, even less ambitiously, on the feasibility of satisfying the Pareto criterion through such institutions. (This criterion says that a social arrangement A is better than an alternative B if some affected parties prefer A and none prefers B: those who do not prefer A, if there are any, are indifferent between A and B.) On the side of political science questions of feasibility ceased to have any prominence. True, some Marxist scholars argued that socio-economic constraints were such – in particular, the state was so closely tied to the interests of the ruling class – that only a capitalist state was feasible in pre-revolutionary modern society, but feasibility analysis of this kind was rarely done in detail; and anyhow it was a minority preoccupation.

The upshot of these developments was that by mid-century the discipline of political theory had all but withered, replaced in most curricula by the history of political thought and the analysis of political concepts. It may be significant that among western countries in the mid-century there was also a high degree of political consensus. Democratic socialists and liberal democrats were never closer to one another, as they all espoused the then orthodox view that while the market was fine in its place, the failures of the market were such as to require the presence of a large and widely ramified state. Had there not been such a popular consensus, the absence of political theory in the academies might have been more conspicuous.

Comparing mid-century with earlier times, it is now quite extraordinary to note that there was no figure or text or even discipline which could have claimed continuity with the greats of the past. There were many students of Machiavelli, Hobbes, Rousseau, Montesquieu, Mill and the like but there were few who did what those thinkers did; few who took up the challenge of political theory. The last great political theorist had probably been Henry Sidgwick. Before the moral sciences tripos at Cambridge had dissolved into more familiar, specialized disciplines, he had used it as a teaching base from which to develop a systematic utilitarian vision of the political, and indeed the ethical, realm.

But if political theory had withered by mid-century, that was also about the time when the first stirrings of a resurgence appeared.

On the side of economics, there were exciting departures, as people began to realize that there was more to the world of feasibility studies than welfare economics encompassed. The Austrian tradition of economics, personified in F. A. Hayek, made a case for minimal government based on the unique power of the market to provide information on people's wants. Public choice analysis, represented in particular by James Buchanan, argued for a similar sort of political regime on the grounds that big government and big bureaucracy are inevitably captured by special interests. Social choice theory, associated with Kenneth Arrow and Amartya Sen, raised problems in the organization of voting which were relevant to many proposals for the design of political institutions. (See Hayek 1960, Buchanan and Tullock 1962, Arrow 1951 and Sen 1970. For introductions to public and social choice see McLean 1987 and Bonner 1986.)

On the side of philosophy and political science, there were also some interesting stirrings. In *Social Principles and the Democratic State* Stanley Benn and Richard Peters (1959) showed just how much work there was to do in systematically thinking through the principles that ought to govern socio-political organization. And in *Political Argument* Brian Barry (1965) brought to the attention of philosophers just how useful the analytical techniques of economics could be in the disciplined pursuit of that task.

But if developments like these were to have any impact, it was essential that someone write the big book: the book which, exemplifying those developments – tackling ground-level issues of desirability and taking issues of feasibility also into account – would make an unquestioned advance on established roads of thought. Only a book of that kind would vindicate and boost the new developments, ensuring the resurgence of political theory that they foreshadowed. As things happened, *A Theory of Justice* played the role required.

THE STUDY OF THE DESIRABLE

The first thing to notice about *A Theory of Justice* is that it breaks cleanly with the preference of philosophers in the previous half-century for the analysis of ethical ideals and principles rather than an exploration of which ideals or principles to advocate. It marks a return to the ground-level study of desirability, in particular the study of what is desirable at the level of social and political organization.

We said earlier that the thing which inhibited other philosophers of the period was the sense that matters of desirability – values – could not be explored in an intellectually disciplined and respectable way. Rawls rejected that inhibiting presumption in the first of his published papers: 'Outline of a decision procedure for ethics' (1951). He argued in that paper, and the argument is endorsed in *A Theory of Justice* (46),[1] that on the contrary there is a systematic way to do this, a way which constitutes the highroad for ethical reflection, both in political theory and more widely.

Rawls's proposed method is best introduced, and indeed

motivated, by a parallel which he draws with the method of logic and linguistics (1951; TJ 19–21, 46–53, 578–82). To develop a logic, at least in the sense in which this is supposed to explicate deductive or inductive habits of reasoning, is to identify principles such that conforming to those principles leads to inferences that are intuitively valid: valid on reflective consideration, if not at first sight. Again, to develop the theory of grammar, as Noam Chomsky in particular has insisted, is to find principles that fit in a similar fashion with our intuitions of grammaticality as distinct from validity. Rawls's proposal is that to develop an ethical theory, in particular the ethical part of a political theory – for short, a theory of justice – is to identify principles such that application of those principles leads to intuitively sound judgements in concrete cases.

The idea is that the mark of a good theory of justice is that it would outlaw slavery and the suppression of minorities, for example, as we are intuitively inclined to do; and that it would support the freedom of speech and the provision of social welfare that many intuitively find attractive. A good theory of justice would explicate and systematize our intuitive sense of justice in the way that logic spells out our sense of validity and linguistics our sense of grammaticality.

This proposal may arouse disbelief, on the grounds that a theory of justice seems to be nothing more then than the reconstruction of political prejudice. But there are two important points which Rawls makes that are meant to undercut any such objection.

The first is that the judgements with which a theory is required to be in equilibrium are *considered* judgements of justice. They are judgements reached after due consideration, free from the influence of special interests and other disturbing factors. This demand corresponds to the similar requirement on the judgements systematized in logic and linguistics, that they should not be our first on-the-spot intuitions.

The second point designed to undercut the objection is that the equilibrium which a theory is required to achieve is a *reflective* equilibrium. This qualification is entered because of the admission, again one with parallels in logic and linguistics, that it is very likely when a theorist tries to systematize his sense of justice that he will find certain considered judgements which refuse to fall under principles that elsewhere fit perfectly well. The qualification means that in such a case it may be perfectly in order for the theorist to focus his further questioning, not just on the principles, but on those recalcitrant judgements themselves; and moreover that it may be perfectly reasonable of him, if he decides that they are the product of questionable influences or instincts, to attain equilibrium by revising the judgements rather than the principles.

In proposing the method of reflective equilibrium for the theory of justice, and for ethics generally, Rawls did not conceive of himself as putting forward something novel or revolutionary. On the contrary, he saw the proposal as a return from the analytical concerns of twentieth-century ethics to the mode of argument found in the great tradition of ethical and political philosophy. He quoted Sidgwick in particular, as someone who saw 'the history of moral philosophy as a series of attempts to state "in full breadth and clearness those primary intuitions of reason, by the scientific application of which the common moral thought of mankind may be at once systematized and corrected"' (51). But though Rawls's work marked a return to classical paths, we hope it is clear just how revolutionary it nevertheless was at the time when it appeared.

THE STUDY OF THE FEASIBLE

A Theory of Justice not only returned political theory to the ground-level study of the desirable. It was also highly original in neglecting established disciplinary boundaries and developing an argument for the feasibility of the particular proposals put forward: that is, the feasibility of the two principles of justice defended by Rawls, which we discuss in

communitarian critique is in many ways overstated, failing to allow for all the moves at Rawls's disposal, or indeed for all the moves he actually makes; and that Rawls's self-interpretation and self-critique is uncertain in direction and, most recently, has taken an unfortunate turn, with the hardening of his aspirations for a political philosophy to end all political philosophies.

This much, representing the general lines of argument in the book, we certainly share. But as is inevitable, particularly given that we favour different political philosophies, our views may sometimes come apart in detail. Before the court of final judgement Pettit is primarily responsible for chapters 1, 2 and 5, Kukathas for chapters 3, 6 and 7; the jury is still out on chapter 4. We have tried to knit our claims and discussions closely together. Were it not for our becoming honesty, we like to think that readers might not have noticed the seams.

For their help in preparing the manuscript for publication we would like to give special thanks to Shirley Ramsay of the Department of Politics at the Australian Defence Force Academy and Anne Robinson of the Research School of Social Sciences at the Australian National University. We are also particularly grateful to Brian Beddie for helpful comments on chapter 7, and to Andrew Williams and the two anonymous referees who read and commented extensively on an earlier draft of the book.

1
A New Departure

> 'No commanding work of political theory has appeared in the 20th century.' So said Isaiah Berlin, writing in 1962 . . . The outstanding difference now, in 1978, is that Berlin's assertion is no longer true. It ceased to be so in 1971, when *A Theory of Justice* by John Rawls of Harvard was published in Cambridge, Mass.
>
> James Fishkin and Peter Laslett, *Philosophy, Politics and Society*

Political theory amounts to nothing less than 'systematic thinking about the purposes of government' (Plamenatz 1960, 37). It raises a number of familiar questions. Should there be a state? What ought the state to try to do? How ought it to be organised? What claims does it have over its citizens? But so understood, political theory has been with us as long at least as western civilization. So why should John Rawls have marked such a new departure with his work in 1971? That is the question we consider in this chapter.

BACKGROUND

By way of background we need to understand the state of political theory prior to Rawls's work. But first it is necessary to appreciate that there are two aspects to political theory, traditionally conceived. It involves the analysis of what is politically feasible on the one hand, and of what is desirable on the other.

Suppose we are members of a group, say a group set up to alleviate problems of poverty in the local neighbourhood, and the question comes up as to the tasks we should take on. There are two natural avenues which we will explore in seeking an answer to that question.

The first avenue will lead us into issues, as we might describe them, of feasibility. We will want to identify those things our group can and cannot feasibly do to relieve poverty, so that we get to be clear about the options we should take seriously. Thus we may decide that the group cannot hope to do anything for long-term alcoholics who live rough and only pass occasionally through our neighbourhood. We may decide equally that the group cannot do anything useful for those who opt more or less voluntarily for a drop-out lifestyle. Those decisions will focus our attention on what our group can do for the unwilling poor who reside permanently in the area.

The other avenue we will then inevitably explore leads into issues of desirability rather than feasibility. We will want to know the sorts of thing it is desirable for us to attempt in helping the local poor. Should we seek to provide financial help and, if so, how much? Should we try to provide help in kind, organising meals and clothing and shelter for the needy? Or should we avoid all such handouts, attempting instead to set up self-help programmes of various kinds?

The exploration of the feasible and the desirable inevitably characterizes any attempt to ask systematically after the tasks which some group or social entity should take on. The lesson extends to the attempt to raise this question about the state and government generally. And so it is no surprise to find that political theory has traditionally been concerned simultaneously with the study of the feasible options of government and its desirable ends.

chapter 3. Rawls argued that his two principles represented a public conception of justice that we could expect to stay in place once put in place. They represented a value which was achievable rather than utopian.

Rawls focused particularly on the question of whether socio-political arrangements that conformed to the two principles would be stable. The first third of the book motivates and presents the two principles; the second third discusses their institutional implementation; and the final third, almost two hundred pages, is devoted to the question of whether they constitute 'a feasible conception' (580): in particular, whether they could serve as a public conception of justice in the stable regulation of society.

One way that Rawls introduces the problem of stability is by reference to the problem of free riding, at the time a problem better known among economists than philosophers or political scientists. This is the problem that while a society of people might prefer to have their lives governed by the two principles of justice than by any other constitution, still each person could find it individually more attractive not to conform himself, trying to take advantage of the conformity of others (Pettit 1986).

Rawls believes that the requirement of stability puts powerful constraints on any conception of justice.

> Just arrangements may not be in equilibrium then because acting fairly is not in general each man's best reply to the just conduct of his associates. To insure stability men must have a sense of justice or a concern for those who would be disadvantaged by their defection, preferably both. When these sentiments are sufficiently strong to overrule the temptations to violate the rules, just schemes are stable. Meeting one's duties and obligations is now regarded by each person as the correct answer to the actions of others. His rational plan of life regulated by his sense of justice leads to this conclusion. (497)

But Rawls is not content simply to mark the conditions

required to secure stability. He ranges widely into the realms of psychology, economics, sociology and political science, in the attempt to argue that the conditions are in fact likely to be satisfied by his two-principles proposal. At this point we see traditional political theory once again in full bloom. Disciplinary and professional constraints are shattered as the study of the politically desirable is reunited with the study of the institutionally feasible. Whatever judgements we may pass on Rawls's conclusions, we must recognize that here is an intellectual contribution of magnificent ambition.[2]

In discussing Rawls's concern with issues of feasibility we have had *A Theory of Justice*, and more generally his earlier work, in view. It is only in chapter 6 below that we turn to the more recent Rawls. But in this context it may be worth mentioning that feasibility constraints bulk even larger in the later work. In *A Theory of Justice*, as we shall see, Rawls is somewhat ambivalent on the issue of whether other visions than his own are feasible too. He implies that they are when he argues for the *greater* desirability of his own vision; but some of his comments in passing suggest that he thinks otherwise. In the later work he moves more and more towards the claim that when the requirements of feasibility – in particular, stability – are fully understood, then we can see that the only feasible candidate for a public conception of justice is at least in the family represented by his two principles. Thus a feasibility argument for the two principles – specifically, for their unique feasibility as a public conception of justice – tends to overshadow any arguments about their desirability.

But if the fact of returning to the combined study of the desirable and feasible marked off Rawls's work from that of his contemporaries and immediate predecessors, it did not distinguish it from the longer tradition of political theory. In order to see what distinguishes the work against that larger background, we must turn to the detail of its method and its message. We do this in the two chapters following. In the second chapter we look at the contractarian or contractualist character of Rawls's theory, in the third at the precise conception of justice which it leads him to espouse.

RAWLS AND MORAL INDIVIDUALISM

Before we leave introductory matters, however, we think it may be useful if we say something on an aspect of Rawls's work which sometimes makes it unattractive to historians and social scientists. This is what we might describe as its individualistic character. The individualistic character of *A Theory of Justice* appears very early in the work.

> Let us assume, to fix ideas, that a society is a more or less self-sufficient association of persons who in their relations to one another recognise certain rules of conduct as binding and who for the most part act in accordance with them. Suppose further that these rules specify a system of cooperation designed to advance the good of those taking part in it. (4)

There are two broad senses of individualism, one metaphysical and one moral. The metaphysical individualist holds by two separate propositions (Pettit, forthcoming). First he says that individual agents are the prime movers of social life, that their agency is not compromised by any social regularities or forces: they are not the puppets of historical process or of any such anonymous social reality. And secondly he says that individual agents are not dependent on their relationships with one another for any of their essential characteristics as agents, that whatever dependencies obtain between them are more or less contingent; the solitary individual may be a conceit, but it is at least a coherent conceit. The moral individualist is a creature of quite a different stamp. He says that whatever their metaphysical status, it is only individual agents who matter in the design of socio-political institutions and it is only the interests of individuals that we ought to take into account in devising such arrangements.

Does Rawls's theory involve a metaphysical form of

individualism? Communitarian critics maintain that it does: specifically, that it assumes that people's relationships with one another are more or less contingent and so takes an atomistic view of how people's identities are constituted. We address that criticism in chapter 6. Does Rawls's theory involve a moral individualist outlook? Here we think that defenders and critics must agree that it does. As we shall see in the next chapter, his approach is based on the assumption that only the interests of individuals are of concern in the evaluation of socio-political arrangements; there are no distinct claims made, for example, by the interests of cultures or groups or structures. Rawls is an outstanding example of a moral individualist.

If Rawls's work is to be taken seriously, we must be able to defend the sort of moral individualism to which he is wedded. We must be able to vindicate the notion that one socio-political system is better than another if, and indeed only if, it advances 'the good of those taking part in it'. We think it is possible to provide an appropriate defence and we would like to indicate how that defence goes; in doing so we draw on other work by one of the authors (see Hamlin and Pettit 1989).

As we have just described it, Rawls's moral individualism is equivalent to what has elsewhere been described as the principle of personal good and the humanistic principle (Broome 1989 and Raz 1986). According to this doctrine, a socio-political arrangement ought to be judged, and only judged, by how it affects individuals; it ought to be judged favourably for promoting the good of individuals – in particular, as Rawls says, 'the good of those taking part in it – unfavourably for not doing so. The doctrine abstracts from how the good of individuals is to be assessed; it leaves that question open.

The quick way of defending moral individualism is to consider the sort of possibility that it rules out. It disallows any appeal to aspects of socio-political arrangements that do not have an impact on individuals in determining which sort of arrangement is best. It ordains that no arrangement can be held to be better than another except so far as it has a favourable impact on the people who live under the dispensation. Stated that way, we hope that the doctrine is more or less immediately compelling. After all, it is hard to imagine anyone arguing for one arrangement over another on grounds which admit that the arrangement does no better than the other by the people involved: on the grounds, say, that it improves the language or culture, or advances the interests of certain institutional entities, though not in a way that makes things better for those people. The people involved – those who are to live under the arrangement – are assumed in this context to be the only ones affected by it; we are abstracting from any effects on people in other societies. And equally the people involved are assumed to be the only sentient beings affected; we may take it that abstract socio-political arrangements are not directly relevant to the fate of non-human animals, or indeed of nature more generally.

The slow way of making a case in defence of moral individualism is to distinguish it from some more controversial doctrines with which it might be mistakenly associated. Moral individualism says that what makes any socio-political arrangement good is that it constitutes or brings about something that affects people appropriately; something, as we may say, that is good *for* people. We distinguish this doctrine from three parallel views. These say, respectively, that what makes an arrangement good is that it constitutes or brings about something that is a good *in* people, something that is a good *by or according to* people, or something that is a good *of* people. We believe that moral individualism must begin to look more or less overwhelming, once it is clear that the doctrine is distinct from those views.

The view that what makes a state or any other arrangement good is that it constitutes or brings about a good *in* people asserts an extreme moral individualism. It says that states are to be assessed by effects within people of a wholly atomistic kind: effects such that those people could logically have enjoyed them in isolation from one another. An example of such individualism is the utilitarian doctrine that what matters is just the pleasure, or the subjective preference-satisfaction, enjoyed by people taken separately. It says that all that matters in assessing a socio-political arrangement is the impact made by the arrangement on such private, subjective feelings.

It should be clear that moral individualism does not entail any such solipsistic view. Being a good *for* individuals does not entail being a good *in* individuals. For all that moral individualism says, the good brought about by a state may logically require social relations between individuals; it may not be something private that the individual can enjoy in the absence of others. The good may, for example, be the good of material equality, or the good of friendship, both goods to which Rawls himself draws attention.

The second doctrine from which we distinguish moral individualism says that what makes the state good is that it constitutes or brings about something that is good *by or according to* individuals: that is, something that individuals explicitly judge to be good. This doctrine will be found plausible by many, particularly those who insist that the state should respond democratically to people's actual perceptions and preferences. Still, the appeal of the doctrine is not overwhelming. It rules out any political philosophy, for example, that praises the state for satisfying rights, needs or other claims that individuals themselves do not recognize at the time.

Again, it is clear that moral individualism does not entail this doctrine. Being a good *for* individuals does not entail being a good *by or according to* individuals. It may be that something's being a good *for* individuals entails that it would be a good *by* those people, that it would be something judged to be good among those people, if they were fully reflective concerning their preferences. But the proposition entailed falls far short of the approach embodied in the *by* doctrine. Clearly Rawls does not endorse the *by* doctrine, for he does not require that people actually all endorse the two-principle arrangement that he recommends.

The third doctrine from which we distinguish moral individualism says that what makes a state good is that it constitutes or brings about a good *of* individuals. This doctrine is less demanding, and less controversial, than either of the other two but it is still more demanding than the moral individualism which we think that Rawls is committed to. The *of* doctrine decrees that the only goods in virtue of which a state can be praised are items that belong to individual people: items like their liberty, their happiness, their equality. It rules out the approval of a socio-political arrangement for the production of goods which, though they affect people, belong in the first place to aggregate-level entities. Examples of such aggregate goods might be the solidarity of a community, the continuity of a culture, or the harmony of relations between racial groups. It is typical of such aggregate goods that while their realization affects individuals, there is no one way in which it affects them all. Thus there is a sense in which they are not goods of people and so the third doctrine would deny that a state ought to be approved for producing such benefits.

We think that moral individualism does not entail even this relatively mild doctrine. A good that is not a good *of* individuals can still be argued to be a good *for* individuals. Community solidarity may be judged good according to the extent that it furnishes goods for the individuals involved even though those individual goods may differ from person to person. When Rawls suggests that all that is relevant in the assessment of a socio-political arrangement is 'the good of those taking part in it', we think it is clear that he does not mean to rule out the possibility that an arrangement should be approved for producing aggregate goods which make a favourable impact on individuals.

We conclude that moral individualism, the *for*-individuals principle, is distinct from the three doctrines which we may describe as the *in*-individuals, the *by*-individuals, and the *of*-individuals principles. Once it is clear that moral individualism is indeed distinct from such approaches, we believe that it ought to be overwhelmingly attractive. Thus we do not think that Rawls's moral individualism entitles anyone to dismiss his political theory out of hand.[3]

SUMMARY

In the next chapter we shall be looking at Rawls's work in the context of the great tradition of political theory. In this chapter we have looked at it in the context of the twentieth century. We saw that the two main concerns of political theory, the study of the desirable and the study of the feasible, came apart early in this century, with the demarcation of philosophy on the one side from economics and politics on the other; and that having come apart, each project tended to wither in isolation: the study of the desirable gave way to the analysis of concepts, the study of the feasible focused on the capacity of the market to produce utilitarian or at least Pareto-superior results. In this context, Rawls's book *A Theory of Justice* had a dramatic impact. There were some stirrings of classical political theory in the couple of decades prior to its appearance in 1971, but it became the testament of political theory reborn. Some contemporary thinkers are unpersuaded about the greatness of Rawls's achievement, arguing that unlike at least many of the classics *A Theory of Justice* has narrow individualistic premises. We concluded the chapter with a partial response to such critics. We argued that the moral individualism presupposed by Rawls is not contentious, as appears when it is carefully distinguished from other doctrines that go by the name of moral individualism.

2

A Contractarian Theory

The contractarian picture presented by Rawls will be familiar to many, for it has been much discussed. Instead of going straightforwardly into questions of desirability and feasibility, he connects only indirectly with those issues, at least in the initial motivation and presentation of his theory. He connects with them by asking after what sort of socio-political arrangement is suitably eligible: what sort of arrangement would we choose, were we suitably positioned to make a choice. The idea is that if one arrangement scores over others on this eligibility criterion, then it is indeed the most desirable of the feasible options.

We should emphasize for readers new to political theory that it was probably the contractarian aspect of Rawls's theory which made the greatest impact when the theory first became known. There were a number of people, most notably the economist, John Harsanyi, who were exploring contractarian approaches at the time but their work was not widely read. To most political theorists, the notion of contract belonged to earlier centuries, being tied to the approaches of thinkers like Thomas Hobbes, John Locke and Jean-Jacques Rousseau. It came to them as a real surprise, even a revelation, that contractarian thought might be put to contemporary use. A measure of the impact made by Rawls's contractarian turn is the fact that there have been so many variations on the approach explored since the publication of *A Theory of Justice*. Some of these are mentioned later in the chapter, in our taxonomy of contractarian methods.

In this chapter we attempt two tasks. First, we offer an account of Rawls's contractarian method in a way that stays close to his own words. And secondly we try to situate that method among the great variety of contractarian approaches which have sprung up in the last two decades or so. In pursuing these tasks we take a more or less standard view of Rawls's enterprise. In chapter 4 however we shall see that there is more to Rawls's emphasis on contract than is recognized in the standard view.

Rawls's contractarian procedure

The motivation for Rawls's contractarian approach is probably fairly obvious. The standard line in political theory is to ask directly about what is desirable at the level of socio-political arrangements; it is to invite discussions about how far liberty and equality and happiness matter, for example, and how they ought to be weighted against one another in assessing such arrangements. But that direct approach often falters, as contributors fail to agree in their intuitions and fail to find a way of arguing out their disagreements. Rawls's contractarian approach offers an alternative path to follow in thinking about issues of desirability. We are not to ask directly about what is desirable and undesirable. We are to ask rather about which socio-political arrangement we would choose, were we able to decide which we could have. We are to introduce considerations of eligibility – considerations of what we would choose – as proxies for considerations of desirability.

In deploying the contractarian strategy, Rawls's first and most distinctive assumption is that when we ask what we would choose, we should be concerned with what we would choose under a veil of ignorance that screens out self-interest. This situation of ignorance is what Rawls describes as the *original position* of contract: OP, as we shall sometimes call it.

> I assume that the parties are situated behind a veil of ignorance. They do not know how the various alternatives will affect their own particular case and they're obliged to evaluate principles solely on the basis of general considerations. First of all no-one knows his place in society, his class position or social status; nor does he know his fortune in the distribution of natural assets and abilities, his intelligence and strength, and the like. Nor again, does anyone know his conception of the good, the particulars of his rational plan of life, or even the special features of his psychology such as his aversion to risk or liability to optimism or pessimism. More than this, I assume that the parties do not know the particular circumstances of their own society . . . It is taken for granted, however, that they know general facts about human society. They understand political affairs and the principles of economic theory; they know the basis of social organisation and the laws of human psychology. Indeed, the parties are presumed to know whatever general facts affect the choice of the principles of justice. (136–7)

The picture, intuitively, should be clear enough. We want to know which of the possible socio-political arrangements is the one we ought to have. In particular, we want to know which arrangement can claim to be just, properly balancing our competing claims and interests (3–6). Well then, we are asked to imagine that we are situated behind the veil of ignorance ascribed, faced with the task of choosing from among the various types of arrangement possible. The idea is that if we can identify the arrangement which we would choose under such a screen, then that arrangement has a good claim to be the just one. After all, it is the arrangement that we would choose were we unable to intrude considerations of our particular interest into the decision-making process.

The contractarian method described is meant to identify

the most desirable of the alternative arrangements – at least in respect of justice – since it picks out the arrangement that we would select under a regime of enforced impartiality. But it is also meant to identify an arrangement that is genuinely feasible. As we imagine ourselves in the original position, we envisage that we are aware of all the general truths about human beings and social organization. The arrangement that we would choose there, assuming that we choose sensibly, must be one that would seem feasible in the light of that general information. Whereas the contractarian method promises to be particularly helpful in picking out the desirable arrangement, of course, it is not going to help in such a distinctive way in identifying feasible arrangements. But at least the contractarian way of thinking does not rule out feasibility considerations; and indeed, as far as it encourages systematic thinking, it is bound to bring them to our attention.

This is just to give the flavour of Rawls's contractarian approach. In order to communicate something more detailed about his method, we shall discuss the answers that he provides to four questions which can be raised about his account of the original position. The questions are: 'Who chooses?', 'What is chosen?', 'With what knowledge?', and 'With what motivation?'

'Who chooses?'

The contractors in Rawls's scheme are individuals rather than institutional persons. But they are not individuals in just their own name; rather they are individuals with close family sympathies, in particular sympathies with their descendants (128–9). The people in the original position then may be seen as the representatives of continuing family lines. Moreover, although this point is only relevant to matters of intra-generational justice, the parties are all drawn from a single generation (140). Rawls insists however that they are not an assembly of all the people living at a given time, even of all the people above the age of reason: to imagine that they were such an assembly, he says, would be to stretch fantasy too far (139).

It scarcely seems necessary for Rawls to insist that the parties in the original position are not an assembly of all the people at any time. After all he goes on to emphasize something which makes the matter of numbers immaterial. This is that all the parties in the OP can be expected to vote in the same way, since each is assumed to be equally ignorant and equally rational. 'It is clear that since the differences among the parties are unknown to them, and everyone is equally rational and similarly situated, each is convinced by the same arguments. Therefore, we can view the choice in the original position from the standpoint of one person selected at random' (139).

What this means is that if you are trying to follow Rawls's theory then you can think of yourself as the only relevant person making the choice in the original position. You only have to ask after how you would decide, since you may assume that others will decide in the same manner. The exercise of contractarian speculation is less daunting then than it might at first have seemed. 'The veil of ignorance makes possible a unanimous choice of a particular conception of justice. Without these limitations on knowledge the bargaining problem of the original position would be hopelessly complicated' (140).

'What is chosen?'

What has to be chosen in the original position is nothing more or less than the basic structure of society.

> By the basic structure is meant the way in which the major social institutions fit together into one system, and how they assign fundamental rights and duties and shape the division of advantages that arise through social cooperation. Thus the political constitution, the legally recognised forms of

> property, and the organisation of the economy, all belong to the basic structure. (1978, 47)

The basic structures between which parties in the original position have to choose are identified by principles, not by particular examples. Moreover, the principles representing the different possible basic structures are presumed by Rawls to satisfy certain general constraints which he describes as constraints of the concept of right. Thus the principles must be general in form, not mentioning particular persons; they must be universal in application, applying potentially to everyone; and they must be publicly recognized as the final court of appeal for resolving people's conflicting claims (130–6).

The assumption that the alternative basic structures have to satisfy such constraints is a substantive one. It means, as Rawls recognizes, that each candidate structure is such that were it legally established, the resulting regime could fairly be described as one which upholds the rule of law (235). The rule of law is contrasted usually with the rule of capricious government; it connotes an arrangement under which everyone is equal before the law and everyone knows where he stands with the law: he knows how he can expect to be treated, if he does one thing or another (Raz 1979). Rawls's assumption in favour of the rule of law is substantive, despite suggestions to the contrary (135). It means that the principles of alternative basic structures have to be judged according to whether they can satisfy, say, the publicity condition: whether they can be publicly recognized as the final court of appeal for resolving claims. We shall return to this feature in chapter 4, when we discuss how far Rawls relies on considerations of feasibility rather than desirability. It means that the issue of feasibility is not simply whether a certain arrangement – say, the two principles proposal – is feasible but whether, in Rawls's phrase, it is feasible as a public conception of justice.

There are two further features to be noted about the basic structure which the parties in the original position are to choose. They are interesting, like the feature just considered, because the fact that the parties pay attention to them means that they consider questions of feasibility as well as desirability. The first feature is that the basic structure is to govern the society of a people with a sense of justice, the second that it is to govern a society existing under the typical circumstances of justice.

That the people have a sense of justice means that, provided an appropriate conception of justice is chosen, they will have the capacity to comply with it; they will not be pathologically driven towards defection (145). The conception of justice chosen will be appropriate, so far as it takes account of the general facts of human psychology and the principles of moral learning. 'If a conception of justice is unlikely to generate its own support, or lacks stability, this fact must not be overlooked. For then a different conception of justice might be preferred' (145).

The assumption that people have a sense of justice goes with the further assumption, also characteristic of Rawls's theory, that if an appropriate conception of justice is chosen, then people will all comply with it; there will not be a significant number of defectors. It is worth noting however that Rawls believes that the first assumption is more basic. He suggests that we may usefully weaken the strict compliance assumption – for example, in considering the theory of punishment – but he thinks that we cannot do without the assumption that at least most people in a society have a sense of justice (575–7).

That the society to be governed by the basic structure chosen exists under the typical circumstances of justice means that the situation is of the familiar kind which gives rise to political questions. 'Mutually disinterested persons put forward conflicting claims to the division of social advantages under conditions of moderate scarcity' (128). The circumstances are not those of a monastery, since people lack altruistic commitment; and they are not those of an Eden, since goods are in relatively short supply. On the other hand the situation is not one of breadline subsistenc either for, as Rawls says in another connection, 'The parties know that the conditions of their society, whatever they are, admit the effective realisation of equal liberties' (152).

'With what knowledge?'

The parties in the original position are under a veil of ignorance about most particular facts concerning themselves and their society. Whatever exceptions there are derive from the stipulation that they know all the facts mentioned in answering the questions of who chooses and what is chosen. But while the parties are under a veil of ignorance about particular facts, they are taken to know whatever general facts affect the choice of basic structure, in particular the facts available from the psychological and social sciences. These are the two important features of the veil of ignorance.

One further point worth noting is that the veil of ignorance is, in a sense, a heavy rather than a light veil (Pettit 1980, 173). Consistently with the desire to have a veil of ignorance which eliminates the effects of bias and self-interest, Rawls might have supposed that in the original position each party imagines that he will be assigned a place in whatever basic structure is chosen – in effect, he will be assigned a personal identity – by a process of random allocation. In fact, what each party is told is that his place under the basic structure chosen will be mainly determined by his own talent and capacity for effort and he is then denied the knowledge of what these are. Under the first, light veil, each party knows the random chance he has of ending up in any position; under the second, heavy veil he is ignorant of such chances, because he is ignorant of their determinants: his talents and related capacities. Under the light veil of ignorance, each person has the same objective probability – the same random chance – of ending up in any particular social position and he knows what that objective probability is: it can be determined by the number of significantly different positions and the number of people to be distributed across those positions. Under the heavy veil of ignorance, people do not have the same objective probability of ending up in any particular position, since the determining factors vary between persons, but no-one knows any of the relevant probabilities. We shall see in the next chapter that this difference between the two veils is of some significance in Rawls's argument.

'With what motivation?'

There are three points to be made about the motivation of the parties in the original position: the first concerns the ends which they pursue, the second the means by which they pursue them, and the third a special condition that Rawls imposes on their dispositions.

As to the ends pursued, the distinctive thing about the original position is that the parties do not know anything about their particular desires, because of the veil of ignorance. They are supposed to choose a basic structure, not out of concern for individually variable goals, but out of concern for desires which they are bound to have, regardless of who they are. These are described as general desires, or desires for primary goods (93, 263). They are meant to be desires for conditions required for the pursuit of any particular goals. Rawls maintains that the primary goods are certain rights and liberties, opportunities and powers, income and wealth, and – something assumed to be made possible in the realization of the others – self-respect (92). These ends are pursued by each party as something he wants for himself and those he represents.

As to the means adopted in pursuit of the ends, Rawls assumes that the parties follow the usual guidelines of rationality, as described in decision theory.

> Thus, in the usual way, a rational person is thought to have a coherent set of preferences between the options open to him.

> He ranks these options according to how well they further his purposes; he follows the plan which will satisfy more of his desires rather than less, and which has the greater chance of being successfully executed. (143)

Finally, the special condition that Rawls imposes on the motivation of the parties is that in making his choice none of them is influenced by envy. 'He is not ready to accept a loss for himself if only others have less as well' (143). This is not psychologically realistic, for undoubtedly we are most of us subject to the temptations of envy. Rawls feels that he may be permitted the assumption on two grounds: first, that to allow envy would be to open the possibility of a collectively disadvantageous system's being chosen in the original position; and second, that the system which is actually selected by the contractarian criterion, the system characterized by the two principles, is itself unlikely to generate strong feelings of envy (144, 534–41).

This gives us a picture of Rawls's contractarian procedure, describing it in a way that still sticks close to his own words. The procedure is a device designed to let us view from a distance the questions that are of ultimate concern in political theory: the questions of which social arrangements are feasible and desirable. It constitutes a novel and engaging way of doing political theory.

OTHER CONTRACTARIAN PROCEDURES

But if the contractarian side of Rawls's work gives it a distinctive stamp and provides us with a useful method, it may also be the source of some confusion. The reason is that contractarian approaches have multiplied in recent political theory and it is becoming progressively more difficult to situate Rawls's method in relation to the approaches of others. In the remainder of this chapter we shall try to situate Rawls in precisely this way. We shall try to highlight the differences between Rawls's contractarianism and approaches such as those of Robert Nozick, Jürgen Habermas, and David Gauthier. (See also Barry 1989 and Hamlin 1989.)

There are two dimensions in which we find differences between political theorists who are or might be described as contractarian. First there are differences on the role of the contract invoked and secondly there are differences on the nature or kind of contract envisaged.

On the role of the contract envisaged by Rawls there are in turn two things to say. First, the contract serves in an evaluative rather than a legitimizing role; and secondly it serves in a heuristic rather than a definitional one.

Suppose that someone wonders why it is legitimate, if indeed it is legitimate, for a state to claim authority over its citizens: say, for a state to claim the right to a monopoly of force or the right to tax. One answer which picks up a long-standing tradition of thought is to say that implicitly, if not explicitly, the citizens have contracted with one another to give those who occupy political positions such power over them. If a contract is invoked in this way, then we may say that it is given a legitimizing role. It serves to legitimize the existence of the state in question, providing it with a pedigree that justifies the various claims it makes on citizens, and does so independently of the content of those claims.

Rawls quite clearly does not mean to accord such a role to his contract. He does not see the contract as something which people have actually undertaken, even if only implicitly. 'The undertakings referred to are purely hypothetical' (16). Thus the contract cannot serve to legitimize the status quo, in the manner of a founding covenant.

The role assigned to the contract in Rawls's approach is evaluative rather than legitimizing. The contract is envisaged as a test of the desirability and feasibility of the arrangement. If we decide that among a range of socio-political options, one candidate would undoubtedly be chosen in the original position, this would show, under Rawls's approach, that the candidate should be the most highly valued. It would show that the sort of state in question, with the claims it makes on citizens, is valuable. It would not show that such a state, if it exists, has a pedigree – say, a basis in citizen consent – that justifies whatever claims it makes. The contract plays a role that has no bearing on the legitimacy of particular regimes.

But if we agree that the contract envisaged is a purely evaluative instrument, a further question about its role immediately arises. Suppose we decide that a set of social arrangements possesses the contractarian property of being the one that would be chosen in the original position. In Plato's *Euthyphro* Socrates asks whether something is holy because the gods love it, or whether the gods love it because it is holy. And similarly here we may now ask whether a set of arrangements, under Rawls's picture of these matters, is just because it would be chosen in the original position or whether it would be chosen because it is just (Pettit 1982).

The question at issue is whether the contractarian property of being such as to be chosen in the original position is *definitional* of what it is to be just, or whether it is a property which merely signals the presence of the independent property of being just: a property which may provide a *heuristic* procedure for identifying just arrangements, but which does not definitionally mean that they are just. Consider, as a parallel, the relation between the property a rod may have of being flexible and its having the conditional property of being such as to bend if put under certain pressure. On one account the conditional property is definitional of flexibility; on another the flexibility is constituted by the molecular structure of the rod, and the conditional property merely signals its presence. Our question is whether the contractarian property relates to justice in a manner which parallels the first account or in one which parallels the second.

The question is important because, depending on how it is answered, the contractarian philosopher will try to justify his method in different ways. If the contractarian property is hailed as definitional, then there is a quick answer to the question of why it should speak for the justice of an arrangement that it would be chosen in the original position:

that is what it is to be just. If the contractarian property is hailed merely as a sign of justice, then the answer will run on different lines: it must involve an attempt to explain why indeed the contractarian property is a sign of justice.

For Rawls the contractarian property is meant to serve as something symptomatic rather than constitutive or definitional of justice. He conceives of the contract he envisages as having a heuristic role. It is meant to provide evidence on which among the arrangements under discussion is the most just but it is not supposed to define *ab initio* what it is to be just. If the argument goes through and people are persuaded to see justice the contractarian way, then they may come to define it in such terms (111). But the contractarian account is not presented merely as a definitional exercise; it is offered as a way of explicating an antecedently identified notion of justice.

If justice is identified independently of the contractarian property in this way, if it presents itself as something already defined in other terms, then how exactly is it identified? Rawls offers two relevant comments. First, and this is merely a preliminary observation, that justice is conceived of as the feature of an arrangement which ensures that it represents a proper balance between competing claims (10). Secondly, and more significantly, that justice is conceived of as fairness; or more strictly, since fairness primarily belongs to procedures, as the property of being such as might have been chosen in a fair agreement (12–13).

Given this aspect of Rawls's theory, it is no surprise to find that he defends his contractarian method, not on the grounds that to be just is simply to be eligible in the original position, but rather on the grounds that any agreement reached in the original position is bound to be fair. The original position is designed by him to meet constraints which ensure such fairness. 'These constraints express what we are prepared to regard as limits on fair terms of social cooperation. One way to look at the idea of the original position therefore, is to see it as an expository device which sums up the meaning of these conditions and helps us to extract their consequences' (21). As he puts it elsewhere, 'The fairness of the circumstances transfers to fairness of the principles adopted' (159; see also 1985, 237–8).

Thus we see that Rawls conceives of the role of contract in his theory as evaluative rather than legitimizing and as heuristic rather than definitional. We have stressed the heuristic aspect of his contractarian theory for a number of reasons. It explains what looks to many like a circularity in his procedure, since it shows the connection between fairness and justice. It lets us see what is wrong with any objection that the original position is unsuitably characterized, say because it is not sufficiently realistic. And it helps us to situate Rawls in the company of contemporary contractarians.

Contemporary heuristic contractarians will certainly include John Harsanyi, who looks to his contract to determine which candidate on offer promises to maximize overall utility; and James Buchanan, who sees unanimous agreement as the only test that an arrangement is Pareto-superior to alternatives: as the only test that it is preferred by some and not dispreferred by any (Harsanyi 1976, Brennan 1987).[1] Contemporary definitional contractarians probably include David Gauthier, who defines what is right in terms of what would be agreeable to rational parties under certain hypothetical circumstances; and Tim Scanlon, who defines what is right in terms of what no-one could reasonably reject as a basis for informed unforced general agreement (Gauthier 1986, Scanlon 1982).[2] Someone like Jürgen Habermas on the other hand does not really come clean on the question of whether the contract he envisages relates heuristically or definitionally to justice (Pettit 1982).

The variations possible in contractarian theory on the role of the contract invoked can be represented nicely in a tree diagram (figure 2.1). At each fork in the diagram Rawls's position lies to the right.

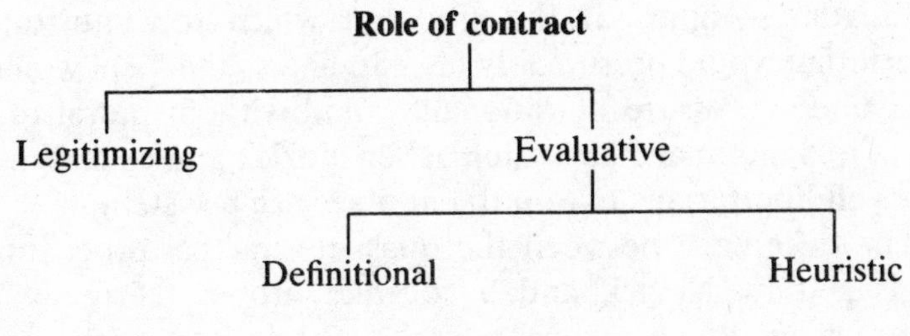

FIGURE 2.1

But the variations on the nature of the contract invoked are even more numerous in contractarian theory than variations on its role. We turn now to these. There are three matters which arise here and therefore three things to say in specification of Rawls's position: that he envisages, first, an intentional contract rather than any unintended quasi-contractual arrangement; secondly, an economic contract rather than a political one; and thirdly, a non-interactive rather than an interactive contract.

The first matter is one on which Rawls's position, and indeed that of most contractarian thinkers, differs from that of Robert Nozick (1974). It may not be quite right, and indeed it runs counter to his own intuitions, to describe Nozick as a contractarian (Nozick 1974, 132 and see Steiner 1978). But his approach is close enough to the contractarian tradition to warrant mention here. As we shall see in chapter 5, he is a believer in certain libertarian rights, a position which makes it hard to see how any state, no matter how minimal, can be justified. He justifies a minimal state system however on the grounds that were people placed under social arrangements lacking a polity – John Locke's state of nature – then the inconveniences of their position, in particular the lack of protection for their rights, would drive them rationally to make arrangements with one another which approximate, without their necessarily foreseeing this, to a minimal state. Moreover, their individually rational choices would give rise to such a system without the infringement – or at least the uncompensated infringement – of anyone's rights. If the situation which the anti-state libertarian would presumably have to hail as the ideal would lead under pressure of rationality, and without moral offence, to a minimal state system, then Nozick argues that this gives all libertarians reason to endorse such a system.

The difference between the quasi-contractual procedure envisaged by Nozick and a contract proper, certainly a contract in Rawls's sense, is that while the parties in Nozick's procedure need have no idea where their individual bargains with others are collectively leading, the parties to a contract proper are concerned precisely with the choice between different collective or system-level arrangements. If they converge on some particular arrangement, they do so intentionally, not as the unforeseen and unintended result of more specific negotiations.

The second question to do with the nature of the contract envisaged is whether it is a political or economic contract. The terms in which the question is phrased are not self-explanatory however and we need to make clearer the matter at issue.

When two or more people seek to make an agreement which affects their interests differently, so that each would most prefer a different arrangement from the other, the agreement may be pursued in either of two ways: one we describe as economic, the others as political. The economic way is for each to calculate what best suits his own interests and then to try to get this: say, to bargain with the other or others, seeking to win the largest benefit possible at the least possible concession from themselves. The political way is for the parties to put aside their own particular interests and to debate about the arrangement that best answers to such considerations – usually considerations in some sense to do with the common good – as all can equally countenance as relevant. The economic approach is institutionalized in the process of market negotiation, the political – at least ideally – in the forum of discussion where the parties are blocked, if only by the sanction of social disapproval, from arguing by reference to special as distinct from common concerns (Pettit 1989a).

Jürgen Habermas's theory is the clearest current example of a contractarian approach in which the contract envisaged is one of a political character (Habermas 1973, Pettit 1982, Elster 1986). He sees matters of justice as determined by what would be agreed to by the parties involved in an act of collective decision, under what he describes as conditions of ideal speech or communication: these conditions are meant to ensure that everyone has the same rights and opportunities of speech, that there are no distorting differences of power and influence, and that the culture is one of radical questioning. A consequence of envisaging the relevant contract in this way is of course that Habermas leaves himself unable to tell how the parties would in fact decide. Thus this contractarian approach does not have the methodological attractions of other alternatives.

Clearly Rawls's notion of the contract is economic rather than political. He sees the parties as each making up their minds by reference to how well the candidate arrangements discussed answer to their personal interests. There is no suggestion that they will step aside from those interests and try to judge arrangements by appeal to considerations of common concern, though of course their personal interests are assumed to incorporate the interests of their family lines.

The third and final question on the nature of contract is whether it is envisaged as a non-interactive or as an interactive exchange. The best example among contractarians of someone who thinks of the contract as an interactive procedure is David Gauthier (1986). In Gauthier's picture the parties are involved in a process of economic negotiation with one another, each seeking to drive the best bargain they can get. The distinguishing mark of Gauthier's work is that he tries to apply and indeed to develop bargaining theory in the attempt to show that there is a favoured solution. In a sense he takes on a challenge put by Rawls, who argues that if the original position generates a bargaining problem, then that problem is 'hopelessly complicated'. 'Even if theoretically a solution were to exist, we would not, at present anyway, be able to determine it' (140).

Rawls's own conception of the contract is non-interactive. He sees the parties as each deciding what to choose without the necessity of negotiating with one another. This conception is not motivated by a desire to avoid the bargaining problem, though he obviously welcomes it on those grounds. As he sees things, it falls out quite naturally once the original position is constrained so as to ensure that any agreements reached there are fair.

We can sum up the different positions on the nature of the contract in a tree diagram (figure 2.2) similar to that used for positions on the role of the contract. As before, Rawls's position lies on the right of each fork.

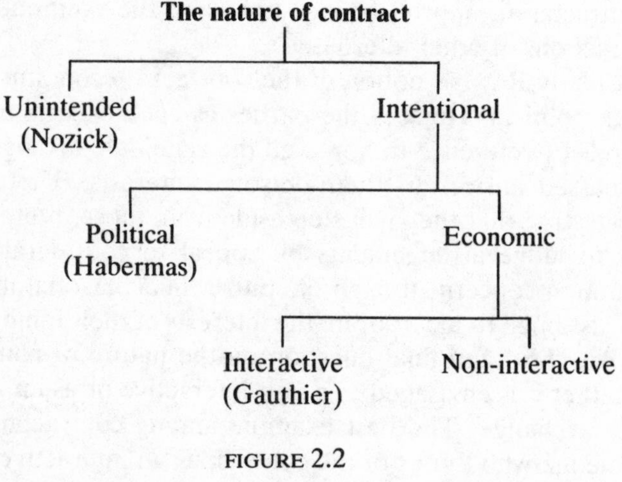

FIGURE 2.2

SUMMARY

In this chapter we have looked at Rawls's approach under an aspect that distinguishes it within the grand tradition of political theory. At least at first sight – we raise some doubts in the chapter after next – the most distinctive feature of his work is the way in which he uses the contractarian device. In the early part of the chapter we offered a fairly detailed characterization of his use of the device. And then in the later part we tried to situate his approach in relation to that of other contemporary contractarians: theorists who, in the main, were influenced by the precedent of Rawls's work. We argued that Rawls gives an evaluative, heuristic role to the contract he invokes and that he sees it as an intentional, economic and non-interactive affair.

3

A Theory of Justice

The task Rawls has set himself is that of establishing what moral principles should govern the basic structure of a just society. We have seen how he thinks the problem should be approached: by asking, not simply what principles are desirable and feasible, but what principles would we choose from an impartial standpoint, concerned as we are to establish arrangements which are both desirable and feasible? We turn now to examine the answer Rawls offers.

That answer, we might note at the outset, is that we would choose to be governed by two principles of justice, the first guaranteeing fundamental individual liberties (of speech, association and worship, among others), and the second ensuring that social and economic inequalities are arranged to offer the greatest possible benefit to the worst-off in society, while upholding fair equality of opportunity. These are the principles that would be chosen by the parties to the hypothetical contract agreed to in the original position (OP).

In this chapter we try to flesh out this answer, giving an overview of the three parts of *A Theory of Justice*. First we consider how the answer was reached, looking at the strategy of choice Rawls thinks would be adopted in the OP and at the general reasons for the final choice of principles. This involves a close examination of the arguments of Part One of *A Theory of Justice*. That done, we shall turn to

Rawls's concerns in Part Two, in which he considers the application of his theory of justice to a range of questions about actual social institutions and practices. We conclude with an analysis of the arguments in the final part of the book, in which Rawls presents a sustained defence of the feasibility of his conception of justice. When these tasks are completed we should be in a better position to offer, in the next chapter, a more general assessment of the character of Rawls's argument.

SELECTING A STRATEGY OF CHOICE

Confronted with the task of choosing principles of justice, the parties in the OP face a particular problem. Given the limitless number of possible principles, how should they go about deciding which principles are appropriate? Rawls makes two moves to render their task more manageable. The first is to stipulate a set of options which includes a list of 'traditional conceptions of justice' as well as his preferred principles; 'the parties are presented with this list and required to agree unanimously that one conception is the best among those enumerated' (122). The second is to argue for a particular strategy which he thinks the parties should adopt for making the choice among these options under the conditions of uncertainty that prevail in the OP. It is this second move that has drawn most critical attention, and it is our primary concern in this section. But we should be clear about the nature of the first move, for it reveals a good deal about Rawls's theory.

The list of eligible conceptions of justice is divided into five categories (conveniently tabulated on p. 124 of *A Theory of Justice*). The first contains Rawls's preferred conception: the principles of justice as fairness. The other four contain classical teleological conceptions (such as utilitarianism); 'mixed' conceptions, which combine principles protecting liberty with, for example, variants of utilitarianism; intuitionistic conceptions (which require us, typically, to balance a list of prima facie principles 'as appropriate'); and egoistic conceptions (such as the principle that everyone is to serve my interests).

Although Rawls opines that the 'merits of these traditional theories surely suffice to justify the effort to rank them' (124), it is hard to see much worth in any of the egoistic conceptions; indeed they seem scarcely describable as principles at all. Rawls does in due course indicate that egoistic conceptions are not to be considered as alternatives by the parties in the OP, since the 'formal constraints of the concept of right' preclude their admission as conceptions of justice. What is not so clearly indicated, but we shall come to see, is that several of the other alternatives appear to be ruled out too, before the parties face the problem of selecting the right conception.

It must be said that the list Rawls presents is a very restricted one. It omits, for example, any form of libertarianism, principles requiring distribution according to need, and desert-based conceptions of justice, to name just three other options. Admittedly, libertarianism does receive some philosophically significant treatment in Rawls's discussion of 'the system of natural liberty' (65–72); equally, desert-based conceptions of justice are later discussed and rejected (103–4; 310–15); and it could be argued that something like 'basic need' is integrated into the two principles of justice Rawls finally defends. (See also Rawls 1975 for his arguments against more radical notions of distribution according to need.) Nevertheless, Rawls's *contractarian* method appears to rule out many conceptions of justice before rational deliberation within the social contract begins. But we leave this point aside for the moment to focus on the OP and the reasoning that goes on within it.

So, how would the parties in the OP decide which (set of) principles of justice to choose? Or should we say, for what reasons would they choose the two principles of 'justice as fairness'? In order to uncover their reasonings, Rawls says, it is 'a useful heuristic device' to regard the two principles 'as the maximin solution to the problem of social justice' (152).

The two principles would be chosen if the parties in the OP adopted the maximin strategy of choice under uncertainty.

The maximin strategy tells us to rank alternatives by their worst possible outcomes, adopting the alternative whose worst outcome is superior to the worst outcome of any other. This is clearly a strategy which would prove attractive to someone with a conservative or pessimistic outlook. The OP, Rawls says, has been so described as to make it 'rational for the parties to adopt the conservative attitude expressed by this rule' (153). In effect, the parties choose principles for the design of a society as if their places in it were to be determined by their worst enemies. This is not, of course, to say that the parties in fact assume that their position is to be decided by a malevolent opponent, since they may not, according to Rawls, reason from false premises. But adopting maximin would be analogous to adopting such an assumption (153).

But why should one adopt a conservative strategy such as this? Before considering Rawls's answer, let us look quickly at other options available. Two deserve mention.

The first alternative strategy or rule for choice under uncertainty is one we might describe as maximax. It tells us to rank alternatives by their best possible outcomes, adopting the alternative whose best outcome is better than the best outcome of any other. If maximin is a strategy for pessimists, maximax is one for incurable optimists.

The second alternative strategy is the maximization of expected utility, as it is usually called. It tells us to rank alternatives on the basis of estimates of probable gain, adopting that alternative with the following feature: if we multiply the gain of each way the alternative may turn out by the probability of its turning out that way and then add up the products, the total sum is higher than for any other alternative. This strategy of maximizing expected utility is neither pessimistic nor optimistic; it goes with the attitude of the rational gambler.

The first alternative strategy is rejected by Rawls for reasons which look sensible and convincing. The maximax strategy is highly risky, and the chances of loss are great. It is a strategy which instructs us to risk everything if there is some chance, no matter how remote, that we will strike it lucky and take the jackpot. A person in the OP using this choice rule might well select principles of justice which ensured a one-person dictatorship if there is any chance that *he* would be the dictator and others his serfs. Maximax does not look to be an intelligent strategy, and Rawls's rejection of it is fairly uncontroversial.

The second alternative strategy is also rejected by Rawls. But this is not quite so uncontroversial. Rawls thinks that there are three reasons why we should reject the gambler's strategy of looking to maximize expected gain, in favour of maximin.

First, he argues that in situations, such as the OP, where knowledge of likelihoods is impossible, or at least insecure, one must be sceptical of probabilistic calculations. It is 'unreasonable not to be sceptical of probabilistic calculations unless there is no other way out, particularly if the decision is a fundamental one that needs to be justified to others' (154). So, for example, while a person in the OP may be able to estimate the gains to be had from being a member of the upper echelons of an aristocratic society, a liberal democracy, or a dictatorship of philosophers, he has no way of telling, under the heavy veil of ignorance, the objective probability of his belonging to those echelons in any of those societies; that probability is fixed by features of his personality hidden by the veil.

We should say that this aspect of Rawls's argument is not entirely persuasive. Even under a heavy veil of ignorance, as we described it in the last chapter, a person in the OP could well reason that given his total ignorance, he should assign himself an equal chance of landing in any position in the society chosen; he should apply what is known as the principle of insufficient reason. Besides, as we saw in the last chapter, there is no deep reason for preferring a heavy to a light veil and under the latter a person would have an equal objective chance of landing in any position. Under the light veil people are assigned identities and positions by a randomizing device; it is not the case that positions are determined by people's objective, unknown personalities.

Rawls's second reason for preferring maximin to the gambling strategy is that, in the OP, 'the person choosing has a conception of the good such that he cares very little, if anything, for what he might gain above the minimum stipend that he can, in fact, be sure of by following the maximin rule. It is not worthwhile for him to take a chance for the sake of further advantage' (154). In short, the conditions embodied in the OP would make contractors happy with the worst available under maximin and disinclined to go for more; it would make them conservative.

The third reason for selecting maximin is that the alternative choice-rules can lead to outcomes which would be intolerable – 'outcomes that one can hardly accept' (154). For example, a non-maximin strategy might lead us to choose an aristocracy as our favoured model of society. Yet this could mean that, if the worst fate befell us, we would find ourselves as serfs in the bottom third of society. This would be intolerable, and we would steer away from any strategy that made such an eventuality possible, let alone likely.

These last two reasons for adopting maximin as a choice-rule are potentially persuasive. Notice that they are clearly reasons which hold only because of the special nature of the OP. It is the features of that special situation which, Rawls readily suggests, 'give plausibility to this unusual rule' (154). And it is indeed an unusual rule which many have suggested requires the persons in the OP to take a unjustifiably conservative or pessimistic stance (Harsanyi 1976, Hare 1978). As a rule to apply under conditions of uncertainty in everyday life, it can lead to absurd conclusions. For example, suppose that subjectively the most probable outcome of our driving to the coast would be that we have a wonderful holiday, but the worst possible outcome is that we are killed in a car accident. The most probable consequence of staying at home, however, would be that we have a quiet time, the worst possible outcome that Uncle Albert visits and bores us to tears with his conversation. Since an ear-bashing is better than death, maximin tells us that we should risk Uncle Albert every time rather than take the slightest chance of being killed. Yet this is counter-intuitive, and any sensible choice-rule should tell us to take the small risk to gain a reasonable benefit. If maximin cannot do this, why should we accept it as a choice-rule?

Rawls has suggested in response to this objection that maximin is a rule which really only applies to certain large-scale choice problems. Its deficiencies in micro choice conditions are, for this reason, irrelevant (Rawls 1974). This does not look persuasive. As Harsanyi has pointed out, it is not difficult to imagine large scale choice problems which maximin would not handle properly (Harsanyi 1976). For example, if the worst possible outcome of the unregulated production and marketing of drugs is some catastrophe, however unlikely, and the worst outcome of regulated production that many life-saving drugs are delayed coming onto the market, maximin would tell us to regulate – even if the expected consequence of *non*-regulation is better, involving more lives saved by the greater production and earlier availability of life-saving drugs. This, again, is less than intuitive.

Yet we should not think this an opportunity to dismiss Rawls. Rather, we should remember what he is trying to do. Rawls should reject the idea that the appropriate principles of choice in the OP are necessarily the principles we most often apply in everyday life, whether in small-scale or large-scale choice. For the OP is a very special sort of situation, designed to ensure that whatever is chosen there is chosen fairly. Being designed in that way, Rawls's claim is that the original position is naturally defined 'so that it is a situation in which the maximin rule applies' (155).

What are the features that make the OP so special that it requires maximin? We do not think that Rawls says enough on this question in offering his case for maximin, though he makes a number of other tantalizing suggestions. One recurrent suggestion which we would like to see developed is that the parties to the OP represent continuing family lines and that this should give them pause about departing from maximin. 'They must also take into account the fact that their choice of principles should seem reasonable to others, in particular their descendants, whose rights will be deeply affected by it' (155).

If it turns out that maximin cannot be justified as a strategy for OP members, it need not mean that Rawls has to accept that something other than his two principles must be chosen by his contractors. Rawls's two principles of justice may still be the appropriate principles to choose, but not for the reasons that the maximin rule suggests. But before we say any more on this question we should, perhaps, turn to look more closely at the two principles themselves.

THE TWO PRINCIPLES OF JUSTICE

From the range of conceptions of justice availabe to them, the parties in the OP choose the two principles which comprise 'justice as fairness'. The final formulation of this conception is presented on p. 302 of *A Theory of Justice*, and we reproduce it below.

> **First principle** Each person is to have an equal right to the most extensive total system of equal basic liberties compatible with a similar system of liberty for all.
> **Second principle** Social and economic inequalities are to be arranged so that they are both:
>
> (a) to the greatest benefit of the least advantaged, consistent with the just savings principle, and
> (b) attached to offices and positions open to all under conditions of fair equality of opportunity.

The principles are presented in 'lexical order', which means that they come in order of priority. In fact, Rawls stipulates two 'priority rules' to make clear the respective importance of the various elements in the two principles.

The first priority rule establishes the 'priority of liberty', allowing liberty to be restricted only for the sake of liberty. The first principle must be satisfied before the second is invoked. Only considerations of liberty are allowed to qualify liberty; thus 'a less extensive liberty must strengthen the total system of liberty shared by all', and 'a less equal liberty must be acceptable to those with the lesser liberty' (303).

The second priority rule establishes the priority of justice over efficiency and welfare. This means, firstly, that the second principle as a whole takes precedence over the 'principle of efficiency', and the idea of 'maximizing the sum of advantages' in society. Secondly, within the second principle, (b), the principle of fair equality of opportunity takes priority over (a), the principle of greatest benefit to the least advantaged (known as the *difference* principle). This means that 'an inequality of opportunity must enhance the opportunities (*sic*) of those with the lesser opportunity' (*sic*), and that, given the requirement of inter-generational justice that a certain level of savings for the future be maintained, 'an excessive rate of saving must on balance mitigate the burden of those bearing this hardship' (303).

The general conception of justice embodied by the two principles, as they are governed by the priority rules, may be expressed in a sentence.

> All social primary goods – liberty and opportunity, income and wealth, and the bases of self-respect – are to be distributed equally unless an unequal distribution of any or all of these goods is to the advantage of the least favoured. (303)

Why would this conception of justice be chosen? Rawls offers two sorts of reasons. First, it is the conception that would survive a critical comparative examination in the OP: utilitarian, egoistic, perfectionist and other conceptions would be rejected, and 'justice as fairness' would remain. Second, justice as fairness has certain 'positive advantages'.

Let us examine these sets of reasons in turn.

Justice as fairness would be chosen in the OP, Rawls maintains, because the maximin strategy would lead to its being ranked higher than any of the available alternatives. This conclusion enjoys a certain plausibility. The difference principle in particular looks to the welfare of the worst-off group and ensures that that group fares as well as possible without endangering liberty. And the lexical priority of the principle of liberty ensures that individuals in the worst position in society cannot be deprived of important liberties. Justice as fairness is thus bound to keep the lowest position within the system higher than the corresponding position in the system organized by any alternative.

Utilitarianism, for example, leaves open the possibility that maximization of utility will lead some people to fare very badly. If slavery were required to maximize average or total utility, utilitarianism would, *in principle*, allow it. So utilitarianism would probably have to be excluded by the maximining members of the OP.

But there is a second set of reasons why the two principles would be chosen in the OP. Justice as fairness possesses several positive advantages, according to Rawls. There are three considerations he discusses in some detail. All of these, in our terms, are considerations which suggest that the two principles are the only really feasible proposal.

First, the principles of justice as fairness are principles that, given the general facts of moral psychology, the parties in the OP can rely on one another to adhere to once adopted. There will be no consequences they cannot accept. Thus there is no risk that they will be asked to accept a lesser liberty for the sake of a greater good for others. We might wonder whether an agreement involving such a risk could be assumed in good faith (176; but see Kukathas 1989b). People who agree to justice as fairness will be able to make the agreement in good faith because they will be able to keep to it and know they will be able to keep to it. Compacts which involve utilitarian principles do not enjoy this advantage, since utilitarianism may require us to do or condone things we would find ourselves psychologically incapable of accepting. 'Compacts of this sort exceed the capacity of human nature' (176).

Secondly, justice as fairness would be preferred because it is a conception that generates its own support and so would be stable. The system it supports is one in which everyone's good is affirmed: each person's liberties are secured, and yet the difference principle ensures that everyone is benefited by social cooperation. 'Therefore we can explain the acceptance of the social system and the principles it satisfies by the psychological law that persons tend to love, cherish, and support whatever affirms their own good. Since everyone's good is affirmed, all acquire inclinations to uphold the scheme' (177). This is not so with utilitarianism, for example, which requires a greater identification with the interests of others and, hence, a greater willingness to accept sacrifices for their good. The facts of human moral psychology make this difficult to achieve; justice as fairness is a more stable conception insofar as it does not depend upon such psychological achievements.

Thirdly, a conception of justice, Rawls says, 'should publicly express men's respect for one another'; in this way 'they ensure a sense of their own value' (179). The two principles of justice as fairness do just this, for 'when society follows these principles, everyone's good is included in a scheme of mutual benefit and this public affirmation in institutions of each man's endeavours supports men's self-esteem' (179). The support given to people's self-respect in turn increases the effectiveness of social cooperation. This provides strong reason for choosing these principles. Again, utilitarianism, by contrast, cannot guarantee a person's self-respect; indeed, in Rawls's view, the principle of utility puts it in jeopardy.

These, then, are the detailed reasons Rawls offers as to why the two principles would be adopted. But Rawls also presents the case for them in what he thinks is a more intuitively appealing way (150–2). We conclude our discussion of the principles with a summary of this line of argument.

Take as a starting point the requirement that all primary goods be distributed equally. This would be agreed to by any person selected arbitrarily insofar as he has no way of winning any special advantages for himself – nor any grounds for accepting disadvantages. It is unreasonable for him to expect more than an equal share, and irrational to agree to less. Parties looking to establish principles of justice would therefore be well disposed towards principles upholding equal liberty and opportunity for all, while guaranteeing an equal distribution of wealth.

But suppose the parties ask: why should this be final? Why not permit some inequalities if these would make everyone better off – for example by eliciting more productive efforts? The thought will lead them to consider moderating the initially attractive egalitarian view. 'In order to make the principle regulating inequalities more determinate', Rawls suggests, 'one looks at the system from the standpoint of the least advantaged representative man. Inequalities are permissible when they maximize, or at least contribute to, the long-term expectations of the least fortunate group in society' (151).

The final step in this intuitive presentation of the contractarian argument is to consider where the parties will hold firm to the initial egalitarian view, and where they will break with it. Rawls suggests that they will draw the line at allowing less than equal basic liberties for the sake of any other good. Thus they will be led towards the conception represented by the lexically ordered two principles of justice.

JUST INSTITUTIONS

Having identified the two principles of justice as the outcome of rational choice under controlled conditions, Rawls is confident that he has derived a conception of justice which is clearly attractive. But that conception is still an abstract notion. More needs to be said to indicate what are the substantive implications of adopting these principles. This is necessary not only to see the practical point of the principles, but also to make clear precisely what they mean. Otherwise, such notions as liberty, opportunity, fairness, and 'least advantaged', which are used to describe the two principles, will remain vague and ambiguous.

In Part Two of his book Rawls attempts to 'illustrate the content of the principles of justice' (195) by describing a basic structure which satisfies them. His intention is to show that 'the principles of justice, which so far have been discussed in abstraction from institutional forms, define a workable political conception, and are a reasonable approximation to and extension of our considered judgments' (195).

The institutions Rawls goes on to describe are those of a constitutional democracy. And although he insists that the arrangements he proposes are not the only ones that could be just, it becomes quite clear that the principles he defends can only be understood as the principles of a liberal democratic society.

In fleshing out his principles in the account of the basic structure of the just society Rawls tries to show how certain basic institutions or practices flow from them. This leads him to offer an account of the just political constitution and just economic arrangements, and to address the question of the nature of the obligation of people in the imperfect world, outside the OP, to comply with the laws of an imperfectly just society. To make clear the link between the principles of justice chosen in the OP and just institutions, Rawls asks us to imagine a four-stage sequence of events. At the first stage, in the OP, principles are chosen. When this is done, the parties in the OP move on to meet in a constitutional convention where they decide upon the justice of political forms and choose a constitution: this is the second stage, in which the basic rights and liberties are made clear. Now it is possible to legislate – to make laws affecting the economic and social structure of society. This is the third stage, when the justice of laws and economic and social policies are considered. When this is complete it remains only for us to consider, in the fourth stage, the application of the rules by judges and other officials.

The four-stage sequence is intended to make clear that the institutions of justice as fairness are just because it can be shown that they would be chosen by society's members suitably constrained by their ignorance of their own parochial interests and attachments. In the first stage, under the veil of ignorance, they would choose the two principles. In the second stage, with the principles of justice no longer in contention, the parties at the constitutional convention are given knowledge of the general facts of their own society – of its economic resources and political culture – so they would choose the political constitution that 'satisfies the principles of justice and is best calculated to lead to just and efficient legislation' (197). And in the third stage, with the political constitution no longer in doubt, and their information more complete, they would choose the welfarist economic and social policies Rawls recommends. In the last stage we view our particular situation with complete access to the facts, the veil of ignorance having been gradually removed altogether in the sequential descent from the world of the OP to our own, and we are able to consider the application of rules with a full understanding of the (just) basic structure of our society.

What, then, are the substantive political and economic arrangements of Rawls's just society?

A just political constitution is one which upholds the first principle of justice – the principle of liberty. This, for Rawls, means that it must be one which conceives of the state as an association of equal citizens (212). The state, under such a constitution, 'does not concern itself with philosophical and religious doctrine but regulates individuals' pursuit of their moral and spiritual interests in accordance with principles to which they themselves would agree in an initial situation of equality' (212). This means that the government has 'neither the right nor the duty to do what it or a majority . . . wants to do in questions of morals and religion' (212).

While the government may on occasion limit liberty, it

may do so only when the common interest in public order and security is at stake, for only on such occasions does 'the government [act] on a principle that would be chosen in the original position' (212–13). Liberty can be restricted only for the sake of liberty. This means that liberty of conscience cannot ever be denied. And when the constitution itself is secure, it means that there is no reason to deny freedom even to the intolerant (219).

The constitution, for Rawls, is to be understood as 'a just procedure satisfying the requirements of equal liberty, . . . framed so that of all the just arrangements which are feasible, it is more likely than any other to result in a just and effective system of legislation' (221). The principle of equal liberty requires that citizens be allowed the opportunity to participate in the political processes of what is best described as a constitutional democracy. But liberty also requires checks on the powers of legislatures. And these Rawls thinks can be supplied by the 'traditional devices of constitutionalism': bicameral legislature, separation of powers mixed with checks and balances, and a bill of rights with judicial review (224). Moreover, liberty requires the rule of law; otherwise the uncertainty of the boundaries of our liberty will make its exercise risky and less secure (239).

A just political constitution is thus one which limits the powers of government, while according it the authority to make and enforce the law. The principle of liberty requires that there be checks upon that authority. Yet it is the same principle from which we derive the government's authority to impose sanctions upon those who break the law, since an ineffective government cannot act to preserve important liberties (240–2).

A just economic order is one which upholds the second principle of justice. A state governed by a just political constitution would thus try to uphold the second of Rawls's two principles through appropriate legislation. Although Rawls does go into the question of justice in political economy, he does not really tackle the question of which economic system is to be preferred, insisting that both capitalist and socialist institutions are *in principle* compatible with the second principle. 'While the notion that a market economy is in some sense the best scheme has been most carefully investigated by so-called bourgeois economists, this connection is a historical contingency in that, theoretically at least, a socialist regime can avail itself of the advantages of this system' (271).

So in his discussion of the economic arrangements of a just society Rawls concentrates on the question of how equal opportunity and the difference principle are to be upheld. He concludes that fair, as opposed to formal, equality of opportunity requires that the government, in addition to 'maintaining the usual kinds of social overhead capital', tries to ensure equal chances of education and culture through subsidized or public schooling, tries to ensure equality of opportunity in economic activities by policing the conduct of firms, and preventing monopolies, and generally guarantees a social minimum income (275).

Economic justice in fact requires four branches of government: an *allocation* branch to 'keep the price system workably competitive and to prevent the formation of unreasonable market power' (276); a *stabilization* branch to maintain full employment and so, with the allocative branch, to help maintain the efficiency of the market economy; a *transfer* branch responsible for dealing with the provision of a social minimum; and a *distribution* branch to 'preserve an approximate justice in distributive shares by means of taxation and the necessary adjustments in the rights of property' (277). Although Rawls does not put it in these terms, it looks as if economic justice is given institutional expression by the organs of a welfare state.

There is one other important constraint. Justice does not permit one generation to take advantage of its descendants by simply consuming its wealth. A just savings principle is a corollary of the difference principle, requiring one generation to save for the welfare of future generations. Interpreted through the contract doctrine, however, there is an upper bound on how much a generation can be asked to save for future people (298).

Thus far, the political and economic institutions of a just

society. The question now is, why should we comply with the laws of a society which, at best, is able only to offer an approximation to the ideal? In the real world, justice is realized imperfectly – if at all.

Rawls's answer to this question is of crucial importance in his account of how his principles of justice might find institutional expression, because it explains how his theory of justice bears on the real world. His answer is that the 'injustice of a law is not, in general, a sufficient reason for not adhering to it any more than the legal validity of legislation (as defined by the existing constitution) is a sufficient reason for going along with it' (350–1). By this he makes clear that what the parties in the OP do when they choose principles of justice is not simply agree to abide by rules which adhere to these principles; they make a more open-ended commitment to enter into a juridical state of affairs. In the OP they ask the question, 'what is a just society', and the principles they arrive at define 'a perfectly just society, given favourable conditions' (351). But they do not agree to abide by social rules only if society is perfectly just, since such a society can never be. They agree to find, and abide by just constitutional arrangements, recognizing that the constitution is a 'just but imperfect procedure framed as far as the circumstances permit to insure a just outcome', and that 'there is no feasible political process which guarantees that the laws enacted in accordance with it will be just' (353).

The contract doctrine, indeed, does not offer us the option of selecting the ideal basic structure; in the OP the parties are confronted with a limited set of feasible procedures of justice. In the end, Rawls says, it is agreed that 'consenting to one of these procedures is surely preferable to no agreement at all' (354). And, under certain conditions, 'the parties agree to put up with unjust laws' (355) – while working for their improvement. We have, Rawls says, 'a natural duty of civility not to invoke the faults of social arrangements as a too ready excuse for not complying with them' (355).

Now in all this Rawls is not insisting that we must obey the law, come what may. While under ideal conditions we can assume that full compliance with the law will be the case, under non-ideal conditions we can assume only partial compliance. Since there will be injustices perpetrated by both citizens and the law, there will be questions of punishment, compensatory justice, and civil disobedience, for example, which cannot arise under ideal theory. Partial compliance theory, according to Rawls, must deal with such questions not just by invoking the principles uncovered by ideal theory and commanding obedience; it must deal with the problem of injustice.

Taking the issue of civil disobedience as an example, Rawls argues that while the natural duty of justice requires us to comply with the laws of an imperfectly just society, the perpetual violation of the principle of liberty and the exhaustion of legal means of seeking redress may justify civil disobedience and, in the more extreme circumstances of repression, rebellion. Then we say that 'if justified civil disobedience seems to threaten civic discord, the responsibility falls not upon those who protest but upon those whose abuse of authority and power justifies such opposition' (390–1).

In all of this there is, of course, a large measure of indeterminacy. In his account of the institutions of justice as fairness, he does not supply any more than a general account of the form social practices might take. But this is all that can reasonably be expected, and it is all that he aims to provide (201). His hope is that by defining the 'range of justice . . . in accordance with our considered convictions' he will single out 'with greater sharpness the graver wrongs a society should avoid' (201).

GOODNESS, STABILITY AND THE SENSE OF JUSTICE

Having established that his two principles of justice are desirable principles to govern the basic structure, and having explained how they might be embodied in the political, legal and economic institutions of the real world, Rawls turns to his concluding defence of justice as fairness. His concern now is to show that his conception of justice would be acceptable to us because it would make for a stable society based on moral principles which uphold our most cherished values. He wants to show that his theory is 'rooted in human thought and feeling, and tied in with our ends' (391). Part Three of *A Theory of Justice* is an attempt to show how the theory gains support when it is examined in the light of a fuller consideration of the nature of *goodness*, and when its *stability* as a moral conception is made clear. Rawls wants to show that his just society is also a good society: justice and goodness are congruent.

To see how Rawls tries to do this, we need to note a distinction he makes between deontological and teleological moral theories. A deontological theory asserts that what is right does not depend on, but is independent of, what is good. So, for example, that we should keep our promises is not determined by the good consequences, if there are any, of doing so; right conduct requires us to keep promises, and this injunction is in no way dependent on the goodness of keeping promises. Promise-keeping is good because it is right; it is not right because it is good or produces good results. Teleological theories maintain that what is right depends upon what is good. If promise-keeping is right, it can only be because it leads to good. Utilitarianism is an example of a teleological theory.

Rawls's theory is deontological because it maintains that respecting the two principles is right independently of whether it produces good. It holds that 'something is good only if it fits into ways of life consistent with the principles of right already on hand' (396). The right is prior to the good. Yet Rawls also wants to show that the right is consistent or congruent with the good: that he is not simply dreaming up abstract principles which conflict with what we regard as good. And that is what the third part of his book attempts to do, offering an argument for the feasibility of his conception of justice which supports the three feasibility considerations mentioned earlier.

In this part of the book Rawls does two things. First, he argues that the parties who select the two principles of justice can be represented as doing so in order to further a weak and uncontentious conception of what is good for them – a 'thin theory of the good'. Acting with 'deliberative rationality', they assume that their good is that which they would choose if they had full knowledge of the effects of their choices, and they conclude that any good life requires a supply of 'primary goods'. The 'Aristotelian Principle', which suggests that, 'other things equal, human beings enjoy the exercise of their realized capacities . . . and this enjoyment increases the more the capacity is realized' (426), helps to specify what the primary goods are. The persons in the OP can be seen as choosing the two principles of justice in order to promote their share of such primary goods. So Rawls thinks his conception of justice is one which is consistent with a concern for the good. A society which is just in his terms is also, in this sense, a good society.

The second thing Rawls does, in Part Three of his book, is to try to show that the just society, as he conceives of it, will be stable and consistent with the good of its members. Why will it be stable? A stable society is one governed by a stable conception of justice. 'One conception of justice is more stable than another if the sense of justice that it tends to generate is stronger and more likely to override disruptive inclinations and if the institutions it allows foster weaker impulses to act unjustly' (454). Justice as fairness is a conception which will generate a strong sense of justice. This is so primarily because of the laws of human psychology which suggest that, if a society's institutions are just, and publicly known to be just, a person will acquire 'the corresponding sense of justice as he recognizes that he and those for whom he cares are the beneficiaries of these arrangements' (490–1). The two principles of justice as fairness Rawls believes are just and of benefit to citizens and those they care about; and furthermore they will be publicly known to be so in any society where they are introduced. Thus they will strengthen the sense of justice and bring stability.

But is the just society as Rawls conceives of it – the society governed by the two principles – going to be really consistent with the good of its members? Rawls thinks so. And he tries to explain why in his account of 'the good of the sense of justice'. In the penultimate section of *A Theory of Justice* Rawls turns to the question of whether the disposition to take up and be guided by the sense of justice accords with the individual's good. Since a sense of justice is understood to be an effective desire to apply and act from the principles of justice, what has to be established is that it is rational for those in a well-ordered society to affirm their sense of justice as regulative of their plan of life. This does not mean justifying being just to an egoist, showing how acting justly would best advance private ends. 'Rather, we are concerned with the goodness of the settled desire to take up the standpoint of justice' (568). Is having this inclination consistent with a persons's good?

Rawls provides three main grounds for the claim that, yes, taking up the standpoint of justice promotes a person's own good. The first ground is that the principles of justice are public and would serve to tie people together, supplementing the bonds of affection and fellow-feeling with 'institutional forms' (571). We could not abandon our sense of justice then without hurting the community – and so, our friends and associates. Granted the laws of our moral psychology (498), this is something we would want to avoid.

Secondly, given that such a society is itself a good in which we would wish to share, preserving our sense of justice would be important. This follows from the fact that participating in the life of a well-ordered society – a society ordered publicly by principles like the two principles of justice – is a great good. Because society is a 'social union of social unions', it 'realizes to a pre-eminent degree the various forms of human activity' (571). Moreover, our nature and our potentialities are such that 'we depend upon the co-operative endeavours of others not only for the means of well-being but to bring to fruition our latent powers' (571). Yet to share fully in such a life, we must 'acknowledge the principles of its regulative conception, and this means that we must affirm our sentiment of justice' (571).

Finally, the inclination to take up the standpoint of justice in a well-ordered society would be consistent with our good because 'acting justly is something we want to do as free and equal rational beings' (572). Indeed, Rawls suggests that the 'desire to act justly and the desire to express our nature as free moral persons turn out to specify what is practically speaking the same desire' (572).

This final claim puts forward a consideration which lies at the heart of Rawls's moral philosophy, and which helps us make sense of his endeavour. What is in our good, he assumes, cannot go against our nature. But how, he asks, can anyone demand that we live by principles of right which require us to subordinate the pursuit of the good to the commands of justice? The answer is that only by doing so can we be true to our nature and be free.

> the desire to express our nature as a free and equal rational being can be fulfilled only by acting on the principles of right and justice as having first priority. This is a consequence of the condition of finality: since these principles are regulative, the desire to act upon them is satisfied only to the extent that it is likewise regulative with respect to other desires. It is acting from this precedence that expresses our freedom from contingency and happenstance. (574)

To be true to our nature, we cannot let justice take a back seat; justice must regulate our other desires, and not be overridden by them. 'Therefore in order to realize our nature we have no alternative but to plan to preserve our sense of justice as governing our other aims' (574). And this sentiment, Rawls insists, 'cannot be fulfilled if it is compromised and balanced against other ends as but one desire among the rest' (574). Many of our aims can often be fulfilled even if they are subordinated to others as circumstances dictate. Not so with our sense of justice. Acting wrongly will thus always arouse feelings of guilt and shame. Such emotions reveal 'the defeat of our regulative moral sentiments' (574–5).

This argument makes it clear that the most important consideration for Rawls is that of whether a conception of justice is one which we, as human beings with an equal capacity for freedom, can live by. A conception of justice which denied our nature would not be a feasible conception for us – and it would not long survive. Such a conception would not command our allegiance. This, ultimately, is the basis of Rawls's rejection of utilitarianism. It is an infeasible moral conception because it misrepresents our nature, viewing us as creatures concerned primarily with desire-satisfaction, and failing to see how important freedom and equality are. Rawls's line of argument in the third part of his book illustrates how large a part considerations of feasibility play in his theory.

SUMMARY

In this chapter we have offered a brisk exposition of the three parts of *A Theory of Justice*. In the first part Rawls puts his case for the two principles of justice, and the associated priority rules, that he defends. This is the contractarian argument that parties in the original position would find it rational – specifically, would find it rational in maximin terms – to prefer the two principles to the rather limited list of alternatives that Rawls considers. In the second part Rawls looks at what the two principles would be likely to mean in the detailed arrangement of social affairs. He plots their impact on constitutional choice, on legislation about economic and social matters and on the behaviour of citizens which the courts have to arbitrate, in particular on the behaviour of citizens who judge that certain laws offend against those principles. In the third part of the book Rawls provides an unexpected, further line of defence for the two principles. Respecting the principles is supposed to be right independently of any good that it produces. But in any case, Rawls argues, the two principles connect appropriately with the production of the good. They are principles which the contractors can be represented as choosing out of a concern for primary, uncontentious goods. And they are principles which ought to generate a stable society, being consistent with the good of the members of the society.

4
A Problem of Interpretation

So far we have tried to present an account of Rawls's theory of justice that is reasonably faithful to the texts. But the account contains elements which are in tension with one another and it is time now to bring this tension to the surface and to see if it can be resolved. The effort is worthwhile because, as we shall see, it motivates a change of perspective on Rawls's work.

The tension we have in mind involves two elements: on the one side, the use that Rawls makes of the contractual device; on the other the feasibility arguments that he uses in favour of his two principles and against alternative proposals. The trouble is that if the feasibility arguments are sufficient to serve his purposes, then it is not clear why the contractual device figures so large in his theory.

Our discussion in this chapter will be in three main stages. First, we review the sorts of feasibility considerations that Rawls deploys and the problem they raise. Then we look at how the problem can be solved by accounting for the role of the contract in Rawls's thought. And finally we argue that this interpretation of its role explains a number of matters that might otherwise be puzzling.

THE PROBLEM

Early in the last chapter we mentioned three detailed considerations, as we described them, with which Rawls supplements his contractual case for the two principles in the first part of his book. We remarked in passing that these all tended to show that the two principles are a feasible proposal, and indeed the only really feasible proposal, for the role of determining the basic structure of society. One consideration was that only the two principles looked to provide for the sort of arrangement that parties in the OP could rely on one another to uphold later. A second was that the two principles option was the only alternative that was likely to be stable, generating its own support. And a third was that the principles appeared uniquely able to give people the sort of self-esteem that facilitates social cooperation. Rawls does not try to prove that his two principles proposal is actually the only one to have these features, but he is insistent that the other major alternatives, utilitarianism in particular, do fail to exemplify them.

The resort to these considerations already raises the problem that concerns us. If an alternative like utilitarianism is unsustainable, unstable or not conducive to self-respect, then it is ruled out in a way that makes little use of the contractual approach. We can imagine the contractors doing two jobs: identifying the feasible options and then deciding which is the most desirable. But whereas the contractual device promises to help us in deciding which is the most fair and to that extent the most desirable social order – it is a useful heuristic – it plays no such distinctive role in facilitating the identification of feasible options. Thus if considerations of feasibility do much of the work of eliminating alternatives to the two principles of justice, it is not clear what important role the contract has within the theory. Is it more of an idle wheel than is generally supposed?

The problem is exacerbated when we consider that most of the third part of *A Theory of Justice*, as we have seen, is also devoted to feasibility arguments. Most relevantly to our purposes, Rawls argues that the two principles of justice promise, and are unique in promising, a political arrangement which is both stable and consistent with people's own conception of their good. Again then, the question is why it is necessary for Rawls to have resort to the contractual argument, if he can display the merit of his favoured conception of justice so much more directly: if he can show that it is about the only conception around – or at least is in the only family of conceptions around – that counts as feasible.

This is the problem for the interpretation of Rawls. But before looking at how we think it should be resolved, there is one important point to make about feasibility. When Rawls argues for the feasibility of the two principles, or against the feasibility of rival arrangements, particularly when he does so in the third part of the book, he is not concerned to show that the two principles would remain in place once put in place, or that a utilitarian regime would fail in this respect. He is anxious to establish, more specifically, that the principles would be, as he often puts it, a stable public conception of justice, and that utilitarianism could never attain that status. Does this mean that it is not feasibility in the strictest sense that concerns him?

No, it does not. Feasibility is a property of possibilities: in the cases which concern us, *valued* possibilities. The question of feasibility is whether the possibility as valued by the two-principles theorist, the utilitarian, or any other sort of theorist, is such as to remain in place, once it has been put in place. Why does Rawls tend to speak of the feasibility of a possibility or proposal as a public conception of justice, rather than its feasibility, period? The answer goes back to the formal constraints on the concept of right that he thinks any proposed basic structure, any proposed principles of socio-political organization, should satisfy. The principles have to be general in form, universal in application and, most important of all, they must be *publicly recognized* as the final court of appeal for resolving people's conflicting claims: they must constitute a *public conception of justice* (130–6). The imposition of these constraints means that the question of feasibility for any proposal becomes the question of whether the proposal is feasible as a public conception of justice.

In introducing the constraints of right in the chapter before last, we commented that Rawls's assumption that they have to be satisfied by any proposal for the basic structure is a substantive one. We can now see one respect in which this comment is borne out. The utilitarian may well protest that his proposal is feasible – so far as no reason has been produced for thinking that every utilitarian regime would have to collapse. But Rawls will be unmoved. He argues, not that every such regime must collapse, but that any regime in which utilitarianism is established as the public conception of justice would do so: it would give way to a regime in which utilitarianism rules but ceases to play the role of a public conception of justice or to a regime in which utilitarianism ceases to play any role at all.

THE SOLUTION

The upshot of these considerations is that the contract is not as indispensable in Rawls's theory as it appears under some interpretations. Once the constraints of right are put in play, then most candidate principles for determining the basic structure of society must be judged to be infeasible. Or so at least Rawls argues. The only clearly feasible candidates remaining, according to him, are all in the family of the two-principles proposal. So why then does Rawls give such prominence to the contract in the presentation of his theory? And why indeed does he play down the role of the constraints of right in reducing the set of feasible options so radically? We have a solution to propose which provides an answer to both questions.

We say that not only does the contractual device help us to identify what we would choose among basic structures –

feasible and infeasible – if we were impartial; it also serves, and serves less redundantly, to dramatize the sort of thing that we should be looking for when we seek out the best basic structure for a society. In particular, it serves to make vivid the constraints of the concept of right, above all the constraint of publicity, which any candidate structure – any feasible option – should satisfy. The constraints of the concept of right – generality, universality and the different elements in publicity – give expression to the idea that any candidate structure must be such that its implementation would involve the rule of law. (We drew attention to this in the chapter before last.) The main role of the contractual device is to keep this fact vividly before our minds.

There are two grounds for making the suggestion, apart from the fact that it would resolve our problem. The first is that if we think of issues of justice in terms of contract, then this does indeed force us to keep the constraints of right, in particular the publicity constraint, in mind. If we think of ourselves as collectively choosing the basic structure, we are hardly likely to forget the publicity aspect – or, for that matter, the aspects of generality and universality – of what we are looking for. The second ground for making the suggestion is that this first proposition is explicitly recognized by Rawls himself.

> It is at this point that the concept of a contract has a definite role: it suggests the condition of publicity and sets limits on what can be agreed to. Thus justice as fairness uses the concept of contract to a greater extent than the discussion so far might suggest. (175)

The picture emerging is a novel and interesting one. Rawls is clearly a contractarian who, as we saw in the last chapter, uses his contract for heuristic purposes. But given that feasibility considerations bulk so large in the argument for the two principles, it is not as indispensable in this heuristic role as it might have seemed. Why does it feature so prominently then? Because it has a second and perhaps deeper role. It is a device Rawls uses to ensure that the preferred basic structure is identified as one which would fully satisfy the constraints on the concept of right, in particular the publicity constraint. If we set out to select a structure in a direct non-contractarian fashion that constraint is unlikely to figure prominently. Not so, if we are forced to select it by arguing that it is a structure that would be collectively chosen under suitable circumstances.

There is a longer way to seeing the importance of the dramatic role played by the contract in Rawls's thought. This is to begin with the publicity constraints; argue that given those constraints, the problem of identifying the best basic structure is a problem of what Rawls describes as pure procedural justice; and then point out that the contractual device is an obvious way to set up such a problem. We shall see how this argument goes.

Because it has to satisfy the constraint of the concept of right, any candidate basic structure must take a suitably determinate form. It has to be

> a system of *public* rules defining a scheme of activities that leads men to act together so as to produce a greater sum of benefits and assigns to each certain recognized claims to a share in the proceeds. What a person does depends upon what the *public* rules say he will be entitled to, and what a person is entitled to depends on what he does. The distribution which results is arrived at by honoring the claims determined by what persons undertake to do in the light of these legitimate expectations. (85 – our emphases)

Understanding the basic structure in this way, Rawls thinks, leads us to see justice in a particular way. Justice is what obtains when acceptable public rules are honoured; the consequent distribution of goods and bads is, therefore, also just – *whatever it may happen to be*. Justice is, therefore, *not* a matter of conformity to some ideal or preferred set of outcomes or pattern of distribution. A theory of justice for the basic structure of society has to be a theory of *pure procedural justice*. 'The intuitive idea is to design the social system so that the outcome is just whatever it happens to be, at least so long as it is within a certain range' (85).

What, then, is 'pure procedural justice'? It is best understood by contrasting it with its alternatives: perfect, and imperfect, procedural justice. Perfect procedural justice obtains when we have both a clear and independent idea of a just outcome and a procedure which assures us of producing it. For example, if it were the case that a just division of a particular cake was an equal division, the sensible procedure to follow would be to let the person cutting take the last piece (assuming, of course, that he is self-interested). Here we have perfect procedural justice: we have an independent criterion for what is a fair division, and we have a procedure that is more or less certain to give the desired outcome.

Imperfect procedural justice obtains when we have an independent criterion for a just outcome, but lack the procedures that would guarantee getting it. A criminal trial is an example of imperfect procedural justice. We know what outcome we want: the innocent should be acquitted and the guilty convicted. But the trial procedures, designed though they are to secure such an outcome, are imperfect inasmuch as they cannot ensure that the innocent will not be imprisoned while the guilty go free.

We speak of pure procedural justice when there is *no independent criterion for the right result*. Instead, there is a correct or fair procedure such that the outcome is likewise correct or fair, whatever it is, provided the procedure has been properly followed. Thus the outcome of a lottery, or of a series of fair bets, is fair – whatever the distribution. What counts as a *fair* bet is, of course, crucial; but the criteria for assessing fairness must be independent of the eventual distribution.

Rawls's idea is that we should see social or distributive justice as a matter of pure procedural justice. There is no antecedent or ideal distribution by which we might judge actual distributions (or the principles we hope will lead to it). Nor is there a procedure that will ensure such an ideal distribution is attained. So the correctness of any distribution is to be determined by the 'justice' of the scheme of cooperation. (Notice that there is no inconsistency between this claim and the claim in chapter 2 that Rawls is a heuristic rather than a definitional contractarian. The contractual device seeks to identify what an antecedent conception of justice requires, albeit a conception of a pure procedural kind that emphasizes process rather than outcome.)

Under pure procedural justice, then, the correctness of a distribution is founded on the justice of the scheme of cooperation from which it arises and on answering the claims of individuals engaged in it. A distribution cannot be judged in isolation from the system of which it is the outcome or from what individuals have done in good faith in the light of established expectations. If it is asked in the abstract whether one distribution of a given stock of things to definite individuals with known desires and preferences is better than another, then there is simply no answer to this question (88).

The problem, Rawls insists, is *not* one of 'allocative justice'. The 'allocative conception of justice seems naturally to apply when a given collection of goods is to be divided among definite individuals with known desires and needs. The goods to be allotted are not produced by these individuals, nor do these individuals stand in any existing cooperative relations' (88). Rawls refuses to make assumptions that would cast all goods as 'manna from heaven', goods which it would be natural to share out 'according to desires and needs, or even to maximize the net balance of satisfaction' (88). What goods there are exist insofar as individuals have created them, and they come into the world with claims attached. These claims are founded on justice, but not on a conception of an independent ideal of a suitable distribution of the goods.

This contrasts sharply with utilitarianism, which does have an independent ideal distribution in mind. Its ideal distribution is one which maximizes average or total utility. The allocative conception of justice, Rawls thinks, leads more or less directly to utilitarianism. And utilitarianism is a theory which sees the basic structure of society as a scheme, not of pure procedural justice, but of *imperfect* procedural justice. If we are to understand the problem of justice in the way Rawls would have us do it would seem that utilitarianism could not be considered an eligible conception of justice.

If the problem of identifying a suitable basic structure for society is a problem of pure procedural justice, then the contractual way of thinking has overwhelming attractions. We design the original position, and the contractual problem in general, in such a way that the choice of basic structure is made under what all must see as a fair procedure. And then we see what would in fact be chosen there. It may be that when the contractual problem is fully characterized, there will be no difficulty in seeing what the contractors would find most desirable among the candidate basic structures. It may be that only a small family of options – the two principles option and some variants – will be feasible. But that will not matter. The contract will not have had much of a heuristic role in helping us see what the contractors would choose but it will have had an important role still. It will have helped us to see what basic structures pass the tests associated with the constraints on the concept of right.

A CHANGE OF PERSPECTIVE

In our account of Rawls's contractarian theory of justice, what matters is not so much the actual contract that would be made as the contractual situation: in effect, the original position. The contractual situation is important because it is designed to ensure a fair procedure and the problem is to see what a fair procedure would require by way of a basic structure for society. It will not matter if the contractual situation, when fully described, trivializes the contract to be made; it will not matter if it leaves only a small family of feasible options. The point is not necessarily to see what would be chosen, as if that were a matter of suspense and excitement. The point is to see what choice would be forced on the contractors by a suitable decision situation: a situation designed to ensure procedural justice.

There are two points which we would like to make in connection with this way of viewing Rawls. These are that it enables us to make good sense of phenomena that may otherwise be puzzling: first, his use of the method of reflective equilibrium; and secondly his presumption, as we see it, against consequentialism.

One may think of moral philosophy, Rawls suggests, as the attempt to systematize our moral capacities. The theory of justice is best viewed as an attempt to systematize one of those capacities: the sense of justice. This is difficult, for it involves *more* than a mere listing of the considered judgements we would render on institutions and actions, as indeed we saw in the first chapter. Rather, what is required is a formulation of a set of principles which, when conjoined to our beliefs and knowledge of the circumstances, would generally support those judgements. From the standpoint of moral philosophy, Rawls says, 'the best account of a person's sense of justice is not the one which fits his judgments prior to his examining any conception of justice, but rather the one which matches his judgments in *reflective equilibrium*' (48 – emphasis added).

This account is consistent with Rawls's view of the 'Socratic nature of moral philosophy': we change our considered judgements when their regulative principles come to light. At times we do this even though principles seem to 'fit' perfectly with our judgements, for 'knowledge of these principles may suggest further reflections that lead us to revise our judgments' (49).

Given this view of the method of moral philosophy, in particular the theory of justice, we might expect Rawls to go for a direct consideration of the different possible basic structures, seeking to pick out that set of principles for organizing society which achieves maximum reflective equilibrium. Why should he introduce a contractual detour? It is common in philosophy of science to distinguish hypothesis-generation from hypothesis-testing. Clearly the contractual device is a way of generating hypotheses about the best basic structure, for as we vary the terms of contract we vary the alternative that would be chosen. Reflective equilibrium, on the other hand, is a method of testing such hypotheses, telling us whether or not the principles proposed fit with our considered judgements. But the generation of hypotheses scarcely seems a difficult task in this area, so why has Rawls invoked the contractual device at all?

We have a ready answer. If the proper specification of the contractual situation is likely to yield more or less straightaway the answer as to what is the best basic structure, making only a small set of alternatives feasible, then we will quite naturally think of the project as one of finding the contractual situation which is itself in reflective equilibrium with our judgments: it will represent the fair procedure we need. And this is just what Rawls does. He sets up the reflective equilibrium process as one of moving back and forth between, on the one side, a specification of the original position and – more or less equivalently – the principles it would yield, and on the other side our considered judgements about the matters involved. If the principles need revision, we do this not simply by changing them but by revising our account of the circumstances – the OP – that led to their being chosen. For example, if the circumstances of choice supply principles condoning slavery, we would be left with the option of either agreeing that slavery might be acceptable or revising the terms of the OP to ensure that such principles could not be endorsed.

We move back and forth between principles and judgements until our account of the OP gives us principles that match our considered judgements. Yet what are continually revised in this process are not simply our principles or judgements: this happens *indirectly*. We revise the various elements in the construction process on the assumption that any lack of fit between principles and judgements is the result of an inaccurate or implausible account of the elements in construction, and therefore of the OP.

But not only does this interpretation of Rawls help to make intelligible his use of reflective equilibrium. The second point we wish to stress is that it also makes sense of Rawls's presumption against a consequentialist way of thinking.

Here it is necessary to recognize something that is not often remarked (Pettit 1990). This is that there is no reason in principle why the property of justice should not be seen as a property to be *promoted* by social agents and arrangements, rather than as a property to be exemplified or honoured by them. With any valuable property, be it something like happiness or self-reliance or justice, the consequentialist view is that things should be done and organized so that the property is promoted: roughly, the expectation is that there will be more rather than less of it. The consequentialist will allow, at least in principle, that an agent may have to act in ways which dishonour the value in order to promote it overall. The judge may have to give a punishment in excess of just desert – an exemplary punishment – in order to ensure that there are fewer crimes, proportionately more convictions and therefore more just deserts overall. The non-consequentialist on the other hand will say that many important values constrain agents, requiring them to honour the values even if this works against their promotion. Thus the judge would be required to refrain from the exemplary punishment and give the offender no more than his just desert, even though an exemplary punishment in this case would better promote just deserts overall.

It is an interesting feature of justice as Rawls conceives of it, that he never imagines that an agent or arrangement should aim to promote rather than honour it. This may be because he assumes more or less full compliance of all parties with whatever principles of justice prevail in a society, so that there is no room for promoting justice apart from honouring it: if everyone else is just, the best you can do to promote justice is to be just yourself. But it is surprising that he never comments on the other possibility. It is as if he assumed, mistakenly (Pettit 1988b), that the contractarian way of identifying justice rules out a consequentialist attitude to justice.

Our interpretation of Rawls's use of the contractarian method explains his neglect of the consequentialist possibility. If any basic structure is required to satisfy the constraints of the concept of right, if the main point of constructing the contractual situation is to identify the family of structures that do, then it is not surprising that consequentialism about justice is ruled out from the start. The point of the contractarian enterprise is not to identify what justice requires, leaving it an open question whether justice should be honoured punctiliously or promoted by the best means to hand. The point is to identify a way of organizing society – a way of deciding what is to be promoted, if anything, and what honoured – which fits with the constraints of the concept of right, in particular the publicity constraint. Rawls assumes, we surmise, that no acceptable basic structure would leave the agents the discretion required if they are to promote certain values rather than honour them; otherwise the structure would not represent the rule of law. Thus he rules out a consequentialism about justice on the same sorts of grounds as he disallows utilitarianism.

One general way of stating Rawls's attitude here, and he frequently resorts to it, is to say that he gives the right priority over the good. We take him to mean by that, primarily, that the basic structures he is willing to consider all tie social agents and arrangements to behaving in accordance with certain public rules, doing what the rules identify as right, and refuse to allow them to be influenced by considerations as to what the good – even the good of having the rules maximally fulfilled – requires. His is thus a deontological rather than a teleological or consequentialist theory of justice.

SUMMARY

In this chapter we focused on a problem arising from our presentation – and indeed from any presentation – of Rawls's theory. The problem is why the contractual device figures so large in his approach if, as he suggests, the only feasible public conceptions of justice belong in the family of his two principles. Our solution was to argue that the contractual device serves to make vivid those requirements on any basic structure that he describes as the constraints of right: these are requirements that the principles associated with the structure be general in form, universal in application and publicly recognized as the final court of appeal for resolving people's conflicting claims. If we think of a basic structure as something that has to be contractually chosen, then we are more or less forced to keep these requirements to the fore, as Rawls explicitly recognizes. Having identified this solution we went on, finally, to show that it provides a perspective on Rawls which explains the connection between reflective equilibrium and the contractual device, and makes sense of his presumption that the two principles should not be seen in the consequentialist's way as a maximand for government to promote.

5
The Libertarian Critique

VARIETIES OF LIBERTARIAN

Liberals can be distinguished into classical liberals and modern liberals (Gaus 1983). Classical liberals of the eighteenth and early nineteenth century asserted that the only role of the state is to protect certain rights on the part of citizens: in particular rights of personal liberty and private property. Modern liberals, who appeared later in the nineteenth century, said that the state ought also to concern itself, even at some cost to liberty and property rights, with issues like poverty, lack of housing, ill-health, lack of education, and the like. Sometimes but not always they claimed that this concern flowed equally with the first from contemplating the demands of liberty, though liberty now understood in more than just the negative sense of freedom from interference (Berlin 1969).

Rawls is clearly a liberal, and a liberal in the modern rather than the classical mould (Barry 1973). It is no surprise then to find that one of the most important types of criticism to which Rawls's theory has been subjected stems from the stable of classical liberalism. Nowadays classical liberals are known as libertarians and our concern in this chapter is with the libertarian critique of Rawls's theory.

Libertarians agree in supporting, at most, a minimal state. Specifically, 'the night-watchman state of classical liberal theory, limited to the functions of protecting all its citizens against violence, theft, and fraud, and to the enforcement of contracts, and so on' (Nozick 1974, 26). We say that at most they defend the minimal state, as some libertarians reject the state altogether. Our only interest is in those libertarians who support the minimal state and these divide into two broad groups, the pragmatic and the principled libertarians.

Pragmatic libertarians defend the minimal state, not on the grounds that the rights which it protects are sacrosanct, but because a dispensation which restricts itself to the protection of such rights has certain other merits. Some, like F. A. Hayek, say that only a minimal dispensation of that kind would make certain benefits feasible. If we wish to provide for the satisfaction of people's wants, we do better to give the state a smaller role, so that provision is effected through the market using the best information available on those wants (Hayek 1960, Kukathas 1989a). Others say that only a dispensation of that kind promises to promote the production of maximum utility or the satisfaction of the Pareto-criterion: the production of maximum efficiency.

Pragmatic libertarians are certainly going to reject Rawls's theory of justice. But the criticisms they bring against that theory will not be distinctively libertarian. They will take the form of charges of infeasibility, inefficiency and the like. We shall not concern ourselves with such criticisms here, though we do not underestimate their potential force.

Principled libertarians are distinguished from pragmatic by the fact that they take the rights which the minimal state protects to be natural or fundamental rights. The rights are requirements whose satisfaction is a good in itself, not a good for any incidental reasons; and a good of supreme importance, a good which cannot be compromised for any reason, short at least of moral catastrophe (Nozick 1974, 30). For our principled libertarians the sort of state supported by Rawls's theory is bound to seem inherently evil, since it allows redistributive infringements of property rights. We shall look in this chapter at the critique of the theory forthcoming from this corner.[1]

In particular, we shall look at the critique of Rawls's theory developed by Robert Nozick in his book *Anarchy, State and Utopia* (1974). Nozick is the outstanding libertarian, and certainly the outstanding principled libertarian, of the present time. He is of particular interest to us, because his book is devoted in good part to providing an alternative to Rawls's theory.

NOZICK AND THE MINIMAL STATE

The book begins with a statement which marks nicely the starting point of the principled libertarian.

> Individuals have rights, and there are things no person or group may do to them (without violating their rights). (Nozick 1974, ix)

The rights which Nozick has in mind are the rights of personal liberty and private property which we mentioned earlier. The nearest he comes to giving a statement of them is in his account of the state of nature envisaged by the seventeenth-century English philosopher, John Locke; this condition is one where those rights, though they may be occasionally violated, are not at least systematically denied.

> Individuals in Locke's state of nature are in 'a state of perfect freedom to order their actions and dispose of their possessions and persons as they think fit, within the bounds of the law of nature, without asking leave or dependency upon the will of any other man'. The bounds of the law of nature require that 'no one ought to harm another in his life, health, liberty, or possessions'. Some persons transgress these bounds, 'invading others' rights and . . . doing hurt to one another', and in response people may defend themselves or others against such invaders of rights. The injured party and his agents may recover from the offender 'so much as may

> make satisfaction for the harm he has suffered'; 'everyone has a right to punish the transgressors of that law to such a degree as may hinder its violation'; each person may, and may only 'retribute to (a criminal) so far as calm reason and conscience dictate, what is proportionate to his transgression, which is so much as may serve for reparation and restraint'. (Nozick 1974, 10)

Being a principled libertarian, Nozick thinks, not just that these rights should be respected, but also that they should have the status of fundamental and more or less absolute constraints. The three terms in this ascription – 'fundamental', 'absolute', and 'constraints' – all require comment.

That a right is a constraint – or, as he sometimes puts it, a moral side-constraint – means at the least that it is a personalized claim (Pettit 1987). Suppose that someone's claim to X is a right which he has against the state; X may be something like freedom from physical interference. If this claim is personalized, then that means that the state is not justified in infringing it, even in circumstances where the infringement would mean that there will be fewer violations by others of that right on the part of others: overall there will be less physical interference. The right is a trump which the bearer can play if the state proposes to flout it in the name of maximizing enjoyment of that type of right overall. It is his personalized guarantee of protection.

For Nozick the rights which he envisages are not only constraints in this sense. They are also more or less absolute constraints, in the sense that they cannot be infringed for the sake of maximizing any of the usual social goals. Nozick says that infringement may perhaps be justified 'in order to avoid catastrophic moral horror' (Nozick 1974, 30). But obviously he holds that it cannot be justified by the fact that it increases efficiency or security or happiness or any such familiar social objective.

Finally, and perhaps most important of all, Nozick regards the rights that he envisages as fundamental or basic. This means that the satisfaction of rights is a good in itself, not something that is good because of some independent goal that is promoted if rights are satisfied. The good of respecting rights is not derived from any more fundamental benefit; it represents itself the rock bottom of moral thinking (see Pettit 1988a).

But though rights are fundamental in this sense, Nozick thinks they can be provided with a motivating rationale. He sees them as giving expression to the separateness of persons.

> The moral side constraints upon what we may do, I claim, reflect the fact of our separate existences. They reflect the fact that no moral balancing act can take place among us; there is no moral outweighing of one of our lives by others so as to lead to a greater overall *social* good. There is no justified sacrifice of some of us for others. (Nozick 1974, 33)

A libertarian who takes the view of rights which Nozick espouses confronts a great problem when he asks which sort of socio-political system is best. It appears that he must say that any system is unjust if it involves infringing people's liberty or property rights without their consent. And so apparently he must denounce any state, no matter how minimal. After all, even the night-watchman state forcibly levies taxes and forcibly takes over people's right to retaliate against certain forms of aggression. The first problem for a principled libertarian then is to avoid anarchism: to avoid having to turn his back altogether on the state.

The problem is particularly acute if the libertarian wishes to mount an assault on something like Rawls's theory. If a libertarian critique of Rawls is going to be interesting, then it should be a critique, not of any theory defending any sort of state, but of any theory defending the sort of state envisaged by Rawls.

The most original aspect of Nozick's libertarian philosophy is that he finds a novel way of resolving – or at least trying to resolve – the libertarian's problem with anarchism. He argues that if a Lockean state of nature existed – that is, if the anarchist's dream were fulfilled – still, a minimal state would emerge. Specifically, it would emerge under two conditions: first, that people and their agencies act in their rational self-interest; and secondly, that they respect the rights of others, not infringing them, or at least paying compensation when infringement occurs. This argument, as noted in the second chapter, constitutes a quasi-contractarian justification of the minimal state.

Nozick describes the emergence of the state in four stages.

First stage In place of the inconveniences of the state of nature, individuals form or join protection agencies (Nozick 1974, 12–15). Nozick supposes that in the state of nature individuals will first form mutual protection associations with their family and friends, but that these will prove inconvenient, involving everyone in the use of arms, leaving each group at the mercy of the chronic complainer, and being unable to deal easily with differences within the group. Inevitably, he says, the associations will give way to a protection agency which, for a fee, will arbitrate all complaints made by its members and, where appropriate, act in retaliation against offenders, those within the agency as well as those outside.

Second stage One such agency, or a federation of agencies, will become dominant in each area (Nozick 1974, 15–17). There are three possibilities according to Nozick: in a given area one agency wins all the battles; one agency wins in one part of the area, another in a second; two agencies fight easily and often, neither attaining supremacy anywhere. In the first case, the winning agency will naturally become dominant, people in the area having the choice of joining it or not joining an agency at all. In the second, the area will split, people towards one end joining one agency, people towards the other joining the opposing agency, and a borderland getting established in between. In the third case, the two agencies, rather than fight each other recurrently, will cut their costs and agree to accept a third judgment on every difference between them, thus forming a dominant federation of agencies.

In these two stages, rational self-interest proves sufficient to push people towards a minimal state.

> Out of anarchy, pressed by spontaneous groupings, mutual protection associations, division of labour, market pressures, economies of scale, and rational self-interest, there arises something very much resembling a minimal state or a group of geographically distinct minimal states. (Nozick 1974, 16–17)

But the regime that emerges in the first two stages can hardly count yet as a state. 'It apparently does not provide protection for everyone in its territory, as does a state, and it apparently does not possess or claim the sort of monopoly over the use of force necessary to a state' (Nozick 1974, 51). These deficiencies are put right however in the third and fourth stages. In these stages, particularly in the fourth, it should be noted that the desire to respect rights plays as important a part as rational self-interest in the derivation.

Third stage The protection agency may, and will, protect its clients against the enforcement of their rights by independents, when it judges the procedures of enforcement unreliable or unfair (Nozick 1974, 101–8). The reason it may do so, according to Nozick, is that each person has a right to protect himself, or to get his agency to protect him, against the sort of risk involved in independents enforcing their own rights: this, by parallel with the right of the community to deny an epileptic the right to drive in order to protect itself against the risk of his having a seizure at the wheel. The reason the agency will protect its clients against independents in this way is that when protection agencies first appear in an area that agency will win which offers the best policy (Nozick 1974, 114).

Fourth stage The dominant agency must compensate independents for the disadvantage at which they are put, by extending its protection to them or by giving them the means to purchase protection (Nozick 1974, 10–11). The reason the agency must offer this compensation is that the protection of its clients against the enforcement of their rights by independents constitutes a transgression of the rights of independents and demands to be rectified by parallel with the compensation required in the case of the ban on an epileptic driver. Compensation will take the form of extending protection to the independents, because it would be more expensive to leave them unprotected and retaliate on their behalf for each unjustified attack by a member of the agency.

What emerges from these four stages does indeed look like a minimal state. It offers protection to everyone and it claims a monopoly of force in the sense of stopping the independents from enforcing their rights against its members.

Still, there are two important respects in which the dispensation that Nozick derives differs from the minimal state proper. First, it allows independents to enforce their rights against one another. 'The dominant protection agency's domain does *not* extend to quarrels of non-clients *among themselves*' (Nozick 1974, 109). And secondly, the system derived does not tax independents at the same level as its proper members: if it provides protection for them in kind against its own members, it can only tax them to the level of financial cost, if any, that would have been involved in their protecting themselves (Nozick 1974, 112). This second feature may suggest that everyone will try to free-ride by opting for independent status but the first feature explains why this won't happen: people will join up in order to be protected against independents (Nozick 1974, 113).

We may agree that Nozick's argument provides a justification of sorts for the type of system derived: the minimal quasi-state, we might call it. But it is important to recognize that the minimal state ordinarily envisaged by libertarians does not allow people to choose between a client and independent status and so does not enjoy the justification accruing to the minimal quasi-state. No one is allowed to enforce all his rights against anyone else and everyone is subjected to the same tax regime, whatever its nature: whether it be flat, proportional or progressive. Thus the minimal state must still offend against the libertarian's strictures. It does not respect the rights which the libertarian cherishes.

This is an important observation but we shall ignore it in what follows, taking the minimal state to be as justified as its quasi-state counterpart. Putting the difference between those two regimes aside, what Nozick's argument shows is that if someone is happy with the type of dispensation represented by the Lockean state of nature, then equally he ought to be happy with the minimal type of arrangement. He may denounce the particular holdings of property enjoyed by people in a minimal state, for these may be the result of past injustices. But he cannot criticize the kind of arrangement which the state represents.

HISTORICAL AND STRUCTURAL JUSTICE

It is at this point that a contrast appears between the minimal state and the type of state which Rawls's theory would support. Unsurprisingly, the more than minimal state is not capable of being derived under the same conditions as generate the derivation of the minimal. Hence the libertarian cannot be reconciled to it in the way he is reconciled to the minimal polity.

The crucial difference between the minimal state and the state favoured by Rawls's theory – for short, the redistributive state – is that the first is guided solely by an historical conception of justice, the second by a structural one (Nozick 1974, 153). Nozick's discussion of this distinction is of great interest in itself but it serves in particular to throw useful light on Rawls's theory.

Under Nozick's libertarian philosophy, there are three principles of justice in holdings: a principle of justice in the acquisition of property, a principle of justice in the transfer of property, and a principle formulating what justice requires by way of rectifying past injustices (Nozick 1974, 150–3). We may ignore the detail, as indeed Nozick does to a good extent, of these principles. The important feature of the theory is that if it operates with principles only of these kinds, then it represents a historical ideal of justice.

What this means is that whether a given allocation of property is just is determined, not by the character of the allocation in itself – the precise inequalities it involves, for example – but by the history of how it came about. The allocation is just if and only if the holdings in question were initially acquired justly and then at every stage of transmission justly transferred. In order for the allocation to be just it is not merely necessary that it come of a just history; it is also sufficient.

By contrast with this historical view, Rawls's conception of justice in holdings is structural-cum-historical. In order for an allocation to be just, it will naturally have to be generated by a history which is seen by the theory as just; fraud or theft in the genesis of the allocation, for example, will render it unjust. But an impeccable history is not sufficient on its own to make the allocation just. Given the second principle of justice, in particular the difference principle, the allocation must satisfy a structural as well as a historical constraint. It must be such that the worst-off group are better off than they would be under any more egalitarian distribution.

The conflict between Rawls's position and the libertarian standpoint is starkly but elegantly drawn in Nozick. However the libertarian critique, if it is to have any chance of convincing Rawlsians, must do more than merely describe a nicely contrasted alternative to the theory put forward by Rawls. It must identify points at which Rawlsians should be alerted by the contrast to weaknesses in their own theory.

Abstracting from some of the detail of his presentation, Nozick identifies two points of vulnerability in Rawls's theory. One is in the basic assumptions of the theory, the other in the area of its practical implications. We shall refer to the corresponding criticisms as his basic and practical ojections.

THE BASIC OBJECTION

Nozick's basic objection is that whereas the libertarian theory acknowledges, as he sees it, that things are already always owned, the Rawlsian theory treats the goods whose distribution raises questions of justice as manna from heaven: as goods to which no one in particular has any entitlement from the point of view of the original position. 'Things come into the world already attached to people having entitlements over them. From the point of view of the historical entitlement conception of justice in holdings, those who start afresh to complete "to each according to his . . ." treat objects as if they appeared from nowhere out of nothing' (Nozick 1974, 160).

Nozick sharpens this objection in a passage directed specifically at Rawls.

> If things fell from heaven like manna, and no one had any special entitlement to any portion of it, and no manna would fall unless all agreed to a particular distribution, and somehow the quantity varied depending on the distribution, then it is plausible to claim that persons placed so that they couldn't make threats or hold out for specially large shares, would agree to the difference principle rule of distribution. But is *this* the appropriate model for thinking about how the things people produce are to be distributed? Why think the same results should obtain for situations where there *are* differential entitlements as for situations where there are not? (Nozick 1974, 198)

How good is the basic objection? The fact that someone produces something, or acquires it with the unforced consent of the producer, is certainly relevant to the question of who should hold it as his property. We endorse the intuition.

But does that sort of consideration tell as damagingly as Nozick suggests against Rawls? We think not.

The fact that production, and more generally the history of acquisition and transfer, is relevant to the issue of distribution, can be made to bear on a theory of distributive justice in either of two ways. First it may be thought to mean that when the theory elaborates the titles to property and the rights of ownership, the task is essentially one of explicating the precise conditions under which acquisition and transfer are just. This is the way Nozick makes the relevance of history to distribution bear on his theory of distributive justice. Thus, so far as he develops a theory of his own in detail, he concentrates on such matters as how to construe Locke's plausible proviso that something is justly acquired only if there is 'enough and as good left in common with others' (Nozick 1974, 175).

But there is another way in which a theory of distributive justice can take into account the relevance of the history of acquisition and transfer to the issue of distribution. It can do so by elaborating titles to property and rights of ownership which makes that history relevant to the question of who shall own what – though that history only among other things. This is precisely what Rawls's theory does. The theory allows people to claim as theirs those things they acquire in a certain manner, but it will constrain that permission in two ways: first, by defining the rights of ownership so that property is not used, for example, to jeopardize fair opportunity; and secondly, by limiting the titles of property, so that no one shall enjoy having more than others unless their having more indirectly benefits the worst-off group.

The fact that Rawls's theory does make the history of acquisition and transfer relevant to the issue of distribution softens the impact of Nozick's basic objection. Nozick makes his objection seem more telling than it is, however, by a subtle misrepresentation of Rawls's theory. He describes the theory as involving a manna-from-heaven model, as if the parties in the original position first of all deprive people of what they currently own, and then redistribute according to a structural ideal. In fact of course the parties to the contract do not debate about the distribution of goods already owned, so much as debate about how goods yet to be acquired, perhaps yet even to be produced, should be distributed. The manna-from-heaven construal holds out the picture of the contractors debating the distribution of goods already produced and produced therefore without the expectation that their distribution would be constrained by the principles adopted in the original position. Under Rawls's actual model, however, the contractors debate about the public principles of distribution under which production and acquisition ought to take place.

Nozick's misrepresentation of Rawls's theory allows him to raise in criticism questions that are not properly addressed to it. One such question, though admittedly it is not aimed specifically at Rawls, is this. 'Isn't it implausible that how holdings are produced and come to exist has no effect at all on who should own what?' (Nozick 1974, 155). But it should be clear that Rawls does not declare that the history of production and the like has no effect at all on the issue of distribution. He does not think that the history is irrelevant to the issue; he merely responds in a different way to the recognition of its relevance.

In this conflict between Nozick and Rawls, it should be clear that the divide between the two stems directly from the fact that the one thinks that Lockean rights are fundamental constraints, the other doesn't. If you think that such rights are fundamental constraints, as Nozick does, then you will object to the notion of the parties in an original position deciding on the principles to govern the distribution of property. The procedure suggests that the Lockean rights are to be recognized and respected only if they pass the test represented by that contractarian device: in Rawls's case only if they pass the test of fairness. Going along with such a procedure means renouncing a belief in the fundamental character of Lockean rights.

The question to be raised then in adjudicating the strength

of Nozick's basic objection to Rawls, and more generally in comparing the rival claims of the two theories, is whether or not it is reasonable to postulate fundamental rights in the manner of Nozick. We do not offer a detailed judgment on that major question here but it may be appropriate to outline one sort of argument which might be plausibly offered in defence of Rawls's point of view, or at least against Nozick's.

It would be fairly reasonable to postulate Lockean rights as fundamental constraints if there were something uniquely appropriate about them: if they stood out, historically or theoretically, as the only serious sorts of rights to countenance. But Lockean rights, as Nozick interprets them, do not stand out in this way. The fact that the Lockean proviso on the just acquisition of property can be variously interpreted shows that Locke himself can be associated with different sets of rights. And a little imagination, nurtured perhaps on the data of anthropology, shows that quite variant sets of rights are also conceivable. Thus the titles to property might include certain community as well as individual titles and the rights of ownership might vary dramatically, depending on how far community interests are allowed to constrain what someone may do to what is his.

The fact that Nozick's preferred rights do not stand out as a uniquely salient set argues against his taking them as fundamental constraints. It suggests that an argument is needed in defence of adopting them rather than any other set of rights and the sort of argument most likely to do the job is one which appeals to a more fundamental value: say, an argument to the effect that the Lockean set promises to produce more happiness, more fairness, or whatever. Nozick himself thinks that his rights are grounded in the fact that they give expression to the separateness of persons (Nozick 1974, 33). It is doubtful however if they are unique in doing this and, even if they were, it is hard to see why they should be preferred on that account to rights, say, which can be held simultaneously to give expression to the separateness and the interdependence of persons.

We have been considering Nozick's basic objection to Rawls, that his theory treats things as manna-from-heaven, and have seen that it derives from a questionable belief in the superiority of a theory which gives Lockean rights the status of fundamental constraints. It remains to consider Nozick's second, practical objection. This does not address the basic assumptions of Rawls's theory so much as its practical implications for social and political life.

THE PRACTICAL OBJECTION

Nozick objects that if Rawls's theory, or indeed any structural ideal of justice, is used to regulate society, then it will have the intolerable effect of requiring the state to interfere continually in people's doings. No such ideal 'can be continuously realised', he says, 'without continuous interference with people's lives'.

Any favourite pattern can be transformed into one unfavoured by the structural ideal, so the charge goes, if people choose to act in various ways; for example, if people exchange goods and services with other people in a certain measure, or give things to them. To maintain a pattern one must either continually interfere to stop people from transferring resources as they wish to, or continually (or periodically) interfere to take from some persons resources that others for some reason choose to transfer to them (Nozick 1974, 163).

Nozick illustrates his charge with the example of Wilt Chamberlain, a basketball player much in demand. He supposes that Chamberlain is in sufficient demand to be able to command a special fee, one to which people who come to see him play willingly contribute. How, he asks, can we look with favour on a theory which would admit that Chamberlain acquires his fortune justly but which decrees that justice nevertheless enjoins that he be deprived of whatever proportion must be removed to sustain the appropriate structural ideal? Such a theory sponsors continual monitoring of perfectly innocent and voluntary exchanges between people to see that they do not generate results that upset the ideal: in Rawls's case, results which offend against the difference principle. It sponsors a society which attracts the elegant jibe that Nozick directs against socialism. 'The socialist society would have to forbid capitalist acts between consenting adults' (Nozick 1974, 163).

But in this objection, as in the basic criticism, Nozick relies for his impact on some subtle misrepresentation. The state which Rawls's theory supports would not continually interfere with people in the manner suggested by Nozick. There is a great difference, and Nozick carefully ignores it, between a rule of law under which it is publicly known that a structural ideal dictates taxation policy and a regime which allows the state to interfere with people as occasion arises. Rawls puts the point forcibly in what is clearly intended as a rejoinder to Nozick.

> Taxes and restrictions are all in principle forseeable, and holdings are acquired on the known condition that certain corrections will be made. The objection that the difference principle enjoins continuous and capricious interference with private transactions is based on a misunderstanding. (1977, 164)

Nozick actually acknowledges the difference which Rawls stresses but he turns from it quickly with a rhetorical question. 'But if some time limit is to be set on how long people may keep resources others voluntarily transfer to them, why let them keep these resources for *any* period of time? Why not have immediate confiscation?' (Nozick 1974, 163). The question is misplaced however. Under Rawls's theory the contractors have to choose a conception of justice to serve in the public regulation of society. It is clear that no party in the original position could look with complacency on the prospect of a state that is allowed to make fiscal raids as occasion arises.

But rhetoric and misrepresentation aside, it is not clear in any case that the alternative hailed by Nozick when he makes his practical objection is really as desirable as he suggests. We may at first welcome the idea of a state which stays out of people's economic lives, short of some injustice in acquisition and transfer. But our hospitality may be strained once we realize that the free evolution of such an arrangement can lead to extremely worrying results. Thus it might mean that future generations are deprived of vital environmental resources. Rawls may have this possibility in mind in the following passage.

> Even if everyone acts fairly as defined by rules that it is both reasonable and practicable to impose on individuals, the upshot of many separate transactions will undermine background justice. This is obvious once we view society, as we must, as involving cooperation over generations. Thus even in a well-ordered society, adjustments in the basic structure are always necessary. (1977, 164)

This completes our discussion of the libertarian critique of Rawls's theory, in particular the critique forthcoming from principled libertarianism. There is a quite fascinating contrast between Rawls's vision and the perspective of the principled libertarian. Great credit is due to Nozick, for having focused on the differences between the two pictures. But the existence of a clearly delineated libertarian alternative does not in itself make for a critique of Rawls's theory. And the basic and practical objections forthcoming from that alternative are not, as we have tried to show, definitive. Rawls's theory remains intact.

SUMMARY

A particularly important critique of Rawls has come from Robert Nozick, the outstanding principled libertarian political philosopher. In opposition to Rawls's theory of justice as fairness, Nozick sets up his 'entitlement' conception of justice, under which only a minimal state is justified. Against Rawls, Nozick raises two main objections: first, that Rawls is mistaken in assuming that goods come into the world unowned and await distribution on the basis of a conception of justice; and second, that a state of the sort Rawls envisages would interfere continually in individual affairs. Against Nozick we have suggested that his objections misrepresent Rawls's argument. Nozick's primary achievement has been to provide the outline of a libertarian alternative, but not to undermine Rawls's theory.

6
The Communitarian Critique

There is another style of politics apart from Rawls and Nozick, which calls down a plague on both their houses. This is the so-called communitarian view, which finds in Rawls's arguments, not simply weaknesses of execution, but a greater inadequacy: a failure to ask the right questions. It contends that, like other liberals such as Nozick, Rawls is preoccupied with the problem of how to derive principles of social justice which might – indeed, must – command the willing allegiance of all rational persons, even persons with quite different visions of the good life. Liberals seek to uncover moral standards by which the social and political institutions of any society may be evaluated. The problem is, the communitarian critics maintain, this task makes little sense given that moral principles can only be understood as accounts of the practices which prevail in actual societies. It is all very well to stipulate abstract first premises ('rights' in Nozick's case and 'freedom and equality' in Rawls's) and then deduce conclusions about what practices are legitimate. But practice precedes theory; and it is hard to see why persons in actual societies should take any notice of such abstract principles or their deductive implications.

The challenge to Rawls here is clearly a fundamental one which questions not just his first premises but his very enterprise. It deserves careful consideration. But one problem must be noted at the outset: the communitarians take as their target not just Rawls but all contemporary liberal writers who share his approach. Consequently, not all of their criticism focuses explicitly on Rawls. While writers like Michael Sandel have offered arguments which take Rawls as the most formidable target of their criticism, others, like Michael Walzer, Alasdair MacIntyre and Charles Taylor, develop their cases without presenting any sustained analysis of *A Theory of Justice*. Nonetheless, we shall try to incorporate their implicit objections to Rawls in our discussion of the communitarian critique.

We open our discussion with a general account of the target of communitarian criticism: liberalism. In the last chapter we looked at differences in the regimes, minimal or otherwise, that liberals support; here we will look at the motivating ideas that they share. We turn then to examine the particular criticisms of Rawls advanced by two of the most prominent critics: Michael Sandel and Michael Walzer. From here we should be in a position to assess the force of the communitarian critique of liberalism, and of Rawlsian liberalism in particular.

LIBERALISM

The theories of justice we have looked at so far – those of Rawls and Nozick – are liberal theories. They assume or argue that the good society is not one governed by particular common ends or goals. The good society is, rather, a framework of rights or liberties or duties within which people may pursue their separate ends, individually or in voluntary association. The good society is governed by law and, as such, is regulated by right principles or principles of justice. These principles are discoverable and statable. And they are principles which do not themselves presuppose the rightness or betterness of any particular way of life (Dworkin 1978). This does not imply that liberals are sceptics who deny that some ways of life are better or worse than others.

But they emphasize that no one should have forced upon him one particular conception of the good life. Some argue that the point of preserving the rights and liberties which liberals cherish is that they serve our most important interest: the interest in leading a good life (Kymlicka 1988, 184).

Liberalism might be seen as one important philosophical response to the pluralism that characterizes the modern world. Given the multiplicity of religious and moral values in modern societies in which a variety of conceptions of the good compete for allegiance, some have despaired of a theory of the good that might be embraced by all. The liberal response has been to advocate toleration, so far as is possible, of different ways of living. This response has taken several forms. The utilitarian approach has sought to go to the higher order good of pleasure and desire-satisfaction as a way of resolving conflicts among competing claims. Various liberty philosophies, on the other hand, have tried defining the good in a way which does not make objectionable assumptions about first order goods; they have advocated only the good of negative liberty (Pettit 1989b). A third approach, exemplified in the philosophies of Kant and Rawls, tries to avoid talk of the good altogether, defining the right independently.

Liberal arguments have, particularly since the nineteenth century, been subject to considerable criticism by thinkers who reject the liberal idea of a pluralistic social order in which the forces of division and conflict are kept in check by a stable system of laws. In the work of Rousseau, Hegel and Marx in particular we find a rejection of liberalism's 'modernist premises', and an attempt to replace the liberal idea of a pluralistic, secular society with a more communitarian ideal of an organic, and spiritually unified social order: 'division, conflict, and competition were supplanted by the ideal of a uniform and common culture which integrates and harmonizes the interests of the individual and the community' (Seidman 1985, 51).

Modern communitarian criticisms of liberalism, in this

regard, are not new. Many of them revive nineteenth-century criticisms of Kant, although the persons targeted have now changed. While it may be going too far to complain 'how distressingly recurrent and hackneyed is a certain pattern of illiberal thought' (Larmore 1987, 93), it is clear that modern objections to liberalism have a long history.

The critics of liberalism argue that a society composed of a diversity of moral traditions, embracing different values, and united only by liberal principles or norms, is no kind of society at all. They doubt that society can be governed by liberal justice. They doubt that liberal justice is a coherent ideal. The practical implausibility of liberal justice, they aver, lies in its philosophical inadequacy.

The alternative they point to is not a society governed by norms regulating individual conduct in a way which leaves people free to choose their own ways of life. Rather, it is a society governed by a concern for the common good, in which the good of community itself is pre-eminent. This comes hand in hand with a rejection of the idea that justice is the first virtue of social institutions.

For the communitarians, morality is something which is rooted in practice – in the particular practices of actual communities. So the idea of looking to uncover abstract principles of morality by which to evaluate or re-design existing societies is an implausible one. There are no universal principles of morality or justice discoverable by reason. The foundations of morals lie not in philosophy but in politics.

Unsurprisingly, these critics have little regard for contractarian arguments looking to scrutinize society's arrangements from some idealized standpoint. But they also reject the idea that procedural justice alone can provide an adequate basis for social institutions. To know what rules or laws are appropriate for us we need to look more closely at our own community and moral tradition to discover what our values are – and what is necessary to protect them.

At the furthest extreme, these critics put a more damning

charge still against liberalism. Three centuries of liberal discourse, argues Alasdair MacIntyre has led to the destruction of that tradition of European moral theory which once formed the basis of our political communities. In the liberal world, the dereliction of the tradition of the virtues has left us with no means for the rational resolution of our disputes. The work of philosophers like Rawls, far from fulfilling a promise to supply the foundations of moral and political argument, simply reveals the absence of agreement about the ethical basis of our practice (MacIntyre 1986).

How telling are these criticisms as objections to Rawls? It is time to turn to this question. But it should now be clear that what is at issue is not simply Rawls's theory of justice, but the philosophy of liberalism more generally. We shall begin our inquiry with a closer look at one of Rawls's most important critics, though this is not where our investigations end.

Sandel's critique of Rawls

In *Liberalism and the Limits of Justice* Michael Sandel offers us a critique of Rawls's political philosophy which, he thinks, identifies what is wrong with liberalism generally. The essence of Sandel's argument is this. For liberals like Rawls, justice is the first virtue of social institutions. But for this to be the case, certain things must be true of us: we must be 'creatures of a certain kind, related to human circumstances in a certain way' (Sandel 1982, 175). We must be persons independent of our particular interests and attachments, capable of standing back to survey, assess, and revise them. Yet we cannot plausibly regard ourselves in this way. In the real world, we cannot detach ourselves from the interests and the loyalties which not only determine our obligations but also establish our identities. Liberals like Rawls insist that we so detach ourselves in order to identify the principles by which to order our association, and maintain that we should judge that association by its conformity with right principles. In so doing we live by a morality we choose or construct for ourselves, and so are free. But this claim makes no sense, for it presupposes a capacity we do not have: the capacity to choose or construct a morality without self-knowledge or, indeed, moral experience. Rawlsian arguments maintaining the primacy of justice rely on a conception of the self that makes no sense and which, therefore, cannot supply the foundations for evaluating our social institutions or moral practices.

Let us look more closely at Sandel's argument. In defending the primacy of justice, Sandel claims, Rawls maintains the priority of the right over the good. Relations among individuals or persons pursuing their various ends are thus to be regulated by a conception of right or justice, and not left, say, to the vicissitudes of politics. Implicit in this view, Sandel points out, is the assumption that there are indeed 'selves' who exist prior to their 'ends'. Rawls himself recognizes this when he writes that 'the self is prior to the ends which are affirmed by it' (560). And Sandel comments that

> The priority of the self over its ends means that I am not merely the passive receptacle of the accumulated aims, attributes, and purposes thrown up by experience, not simply a product of the vagaries of circumstance, but always, irreducibly, an active, willing agent, distinguishable from my surroundings, and capable of choice. (Sandel 1982, 19)

Now there are two senses in which the self might be prior to its ends in Sandel's view. In the first, 'moral' sense the self must be regarded as prior to the ends it chooses if it is to be seen as autonomous, and if it is to be accorded the respect due to the person viewed 'as the bearer of a dignity beyond the roles that he inhabits and the ends he may pursue' (Sandel 1982, 20). In the second sense, the self must be prior to the ends it affirms inasmuch as it must be 'independently identifiable' (Sandel 1982, 20). This, according to Sandel, is an epistemological requirement. And he thinks it important for Rawls that we are able to identify the self in this way.

Rawls insists, in Sandel's words, that the self should be seen as something more than 'a concatenation of various contingent desires, wants, and needs' (Sandel 1982, 20). If that were all the self amounted to, it would be hard to separate the different selves to be found among all the 'attributes' we might see. What is the self to whom we attribute these desires and ends if the self is just a collection of desires and ends? Moreover, if the self is always fully constituted by its attributes, then *any* change in my circumstances would change the person that I am: my attributes are not things I possess but define the person I am. There would be no distinction between the subject and the object of possession, it would be impossible to distinguish what is me from what is mine, and we would be left with a 'radically situated subject' (Sandel 1982, 21).

The problem raised by Sandel is that Rawls's conception of a moral subject as a self totally detached from its empirically-given features is inadequate. Such a conception of the person would amount to nothing more than an abstraction, a 'radically disembodied' subject which is the polar opposite of the 'radically situated' subject (Sandel 1982, 21). Such a subject would be incapable of rational choice. Shorn of all experience, it would lack motivation and have no capacity for deliberation. The price of such complete detachment is arbitrariness. And in the selection of principles of justice, arbitrariness is hardly a virtue.

Rawls might argue that the OP supplies us with an account of the person as a moral subject who is detached enough to be capable of standing back and choosing principles, but not so detached from the empirical world that his choices amount to nothing more than arbitrary selections. He might argue that he goes for a moderate alternative to the extremes of radical disembodiment and radical situation.

The trouble is, Sandel maintains, Rawls does not succeed in finding that middle way. The account of the person implicit in the theory of the OP turns out to be an account of a 'radically disembodied subject', incapable of choice. 'The notion of the person embedded in the original position is too formal and abstract, too detached from contingency to account for the requisite motivations' (Sandel 1982, 27–8).

In Rawls's view, he says, any account of self and ends must tell how the self is distinguished from, and how it is connected to, its ends. 'Without the first we are left with a radically situated subject; without the second, a radically disembodied subject' (Sandel 1982, 54). Rawls's solution, Sandel explains, is implicit in the design of the OP: it is to conceive the self as 'a subject of possession' (Sandel 1982, 54). It is the possessor of its attributes, and of its ends. In possession, the self is distanced from its ends without being detached altogether. The self thus turns out to be a subject whose identity is given independently of the things it has – independently of its interests, its ends, and indeed (because all persons in the OP are assumed to be mutually disinterested) its relations with others. How is the self then connected to its ends and its attributes? The answer is: by choice. The self chooses its ends: it *wills* the connection with them. This is of crucial importance for Rawls's account of the person. 'Thus a moral person is a subject with ends he has chosen, and his fundamental preference is for conditions that enable him to frame a mode of life that expresses his nature as a free and equal rational being as fully as circumstances permit' (561).

Sandel's objection is that this account of the self, and of its connection with its ends, does not stand up. And its inadequacy is most clearly revealed by Rawls's very theory of justice, which is from time to time forced to look beyond that conception of the self in order to develop the conclusions it seeks. Sandel has two points to make here. First, Rawls's person is incapable of *choosing* in any meaningful sense. Second, the theory Rawls defends ends up relying, not on the notion of the self as independently identifiable and prior to its ends, but on an 'intersubjective conception' of the self. Let us take these points in turn.

Why is the person implicit in the OP incapable of choice? Recall that the parties in the OP are asked to choose principles of justice. Whatever they choose, Rawls says, will be accepted as the right principles. Yet they don't really *choose* those principles, since 'their situation is designed in such a way that they are guaranteed to . . . "wish" to choose only certain principles' Sandel 1982, 127). There is very little voluntary about their actions: there is no possibility of their 'choosing' any other principles. Although these parties are parties to a *contract*, who are here to enter into *agreement*, they cannot decide to contract or choose to agree. For one thing, they are not really separate parties at all. Since they are undifferentiated under the veil of ignorance, they are in fact not just similarly but identically situated. Logically there can be only one person in the OP. Any agreement 'they' reach cannot be agreement *with* each other *to* live by certain principles, for there are no others. At best there is only a metaphorical agreement I make with 'myself' (Sandel 1982, 129). The agreement reached here is less the agreement of persons to (choose to) accept principles of conduct, than the agreement (in a quite different sense) of a person with a proposition. In Sandel's terms, contractual agreement in the OP exemplifies not the voluntarism involved in the choice of principles, but the cognitivism involved in discovering or coming to understand what the right principles are. In the OP principles of justice are not chosen but discovered (Sandel 1982, 130–2).

But this is not the only reason the person in the OP is incapable of choice. The self presupposed in Rawls's theory has no capacity to choose because it is incapable of deliberation and reflection in the appropriate senses of these terms, or so Sandel maintains. Rawls says that

> while rational principles can focus our judgments and set up guidelines for reflection, we must finally choose for ourselves in the sense that the choice often rests on our direct self-knowledge not only of what things we want but also of how much we want them. (416)

He also says that a rational plan for a person is

> the plan that would be decided upon as the outcome of careful reflection in which the agent reviewed, in the light of all the relevant facts, what it would be like to carry out these plans and thereby ascertained the course of action that would best realize his more fundamental desires. (417)

In this view reflection presupposes the existence of fundamental desires. And the object of reflection is not the self as subject of desires. For Rawls, 'the faculty of self-reflection is limited to weighing the relative intensity of existing wants and desires, and the deliberation it entails cannot inquire into the identity of the agent ("Who am I, really?"), only into the feelings and sentiments of the agent ("What do I really *feel* like or most *prefer*?")' (Sandel 1982, 159). This is unsurprising, Sandel thinks, 'because Rawls's self is conceived as barren of constituent traits, possessed only of contingent attributes held at a certain distance, and so there is nothing *in* the self for reflection to survey or apprehend' (Sandel 1982, 160–1).

But if the agent's desires are taken as given, the agent's choice of values or ends is choice in a rather odd sense of the word. Since the desires and wants are not chosen but are the product of circumstance, choice involves nothing more than identifying these wants, and matching them with available means of satisfying them. In this sense, 'my aims, values, and conceptions of the good are not the products of choice' (Sandel 1982, 163). I am in no sense free to *choose* my values or ends. Distinguishing between first- and second-order desires does not extricate Rawls from this difficulty with his account of agency. To say that we are capable of forming desires about what desires we are to have does not change anything; while it complicates our estimate of pre-existing desires which now include second-order desires, the 'resulting conception of the good could no more be said to be chosen than one arising from first-order desires alone' (Sandel 1982, 164). In the matter of its most important concerns the agent does not choose but is determined.

It might, of course, be suggested that 'choice' be seen as

the capacity to act independently of the influence of pre-existing desires and wants. The agent might simply 'plump, just arbitrarily, one way or the other, without relying on any preference or desire at all' (Sandel 1982, 164). But Rawls has already rejected this idea. 'The notion of radical choice . . . finds no place in justice as fairness' (1980, 568). Yet if the notion of radical choice confuses choice with arbitrariness and caprice, Sandel maintains, the notion Rawls is left with seems to confuse it with necessity. It is hard to see how the moral subject Rawls has described 'chooses' in any appropriate sense.

This leads us to Sandel's second point: not now that Rawls's persons are incapable of properly choosing but that Rawls is led to rely on a quite different conception of the self in order to develop his substantive claims. Sandel develops this argument by drawing out one strand in the main line of objection raised against Rawls by Nozick; we discussed this objection in the last chapter.

Nozick objects to Rawls's argument for the difference principle, particularly to his assumption that the distribution of natural talents is best regarded as a 'common' or 'collective' possession to be shared across society as a whole. Rawls says quite plainly that the 'difference principle represents, in effect, an agreement to regard the distribution of natural talents as a common asset and to share in the benefits of this distribution whatever it turns out to be' (101). To take this view, Nozick suggests, is to fail to respect the inviolability of persons and the Kantian injunction to treat persons as ends and never as means. In Rawls's theory, this injunction is respected only by pressing so hard on 'the distinction between men and their talents, assets, abilities and special traits' (Nozick 1974, 228) that, in the end, it becomes questionable whether a coherent conception of a person remains – now to be treated as an end and never as a means. 'Why we, thick with particular traits, should be cheered that (only) the thus purified men within us are not regarded as means is also unclear' (Nozick 1974, 228).

Now Rawls does, of course, have a reason for wishing to

regard natural assets as collectively owned. In his view, no one can *deserve* his natural assets or the benefits that flow from them, since the possession of particular talents, or character traits is a matter of luck. No one deserves the endowments he is born with. From a moral point of view, such assets are distributed arbitrarily. To this view Nozick objects that the arbitrariness of assets does not undermine desert because I do not have to deserve to be deserving, or deserve to deserve to be deserving. 'It needn't be that the foundations underlying desert are themselves deserved, *all the way down*' (Nozick 1974, 225). Rawls's defence against this attack is to press hard the distinction between the subject and its possessed attributes – once again leaving the subject stripped of empirically identifiable characteristics and, so, without anything which might serve as the basis for desert. Yet if we accept that arbitrariness undermines individual possession and individual desert, Nozick asks, why should we accept the difference principle rather than the entitlement theory which opts for allowing assets to lie where they fall. I may not deserve my natural assets, but it does not follow either that I cannot be entitled to them, or that they belong to the community.

Now it is true that Nozick says nothing to *establish* any presumption in favour of letting assets lie where they fall. It is a presumption he makes because it is consistent with his first premise: that individuals have *rights*. But equally, Rawls does nothing to establish any presumption in favour of taking natural assets to be collectively owned. Collective ownership is not a conclusion reached in the OP; it is taken for granted there.

Sandel thinks all this is very significant because it reveals something central about Rawls's theory. In defending his position, Rawls is forced to rely on a wider subject of possession than the individual. Despite his insistence that his theory is premised on the view that the self is prior to its ends, and is connected to them by choice, Rawls is continually led by the logic of his position to admit that his argument presupposes the existence of some community of persons. Rawls's only option if he is to answer Nozick's arguments is to abandon the conception of the self he has developed. He can answer Nozick's charge that the difference principle uses me as a means to others' ends 'not by claiming that my *assets* rather than the *person* are being used, but instead by questioning the sense in which those who share in . . . "my" assets are properly described as . . . "others"' (Sandel 1982, 79). This defence 'ties the notion of common assets to the possibility of a common subject of possession', appealing to 'an intersubjective conception of the self' (Sandel 1982, 80). And he can respond to Nozick's challenge that the absence of a deserving subject need not lead to any presumption in favour of the difference principle 'only by implicit reliance on a claim of social desert, and hence reliance on a wider subject of possession, presumably the community, held to own the assets we individually bear' (Sandel 1982, 103).

Why is all this important? Perhaps this is the time to take a step back and look at the bigger picture, so the point of Sandel's communitarian critique becomes intelligible. What Sandel is attacking is Rawls's (and liberalism's) fundamental contention that a community is the product of association by independent individuals, and that the worth of that community is to be estimated by the *justice* of the terms upon which those individuals associate. Sandel, like all communitarians, wants to maintain that it makes no sense to think of a community in this way because the very existence of individuals capable of agreeing to form associations, or assenting to terms of agreement, *presupposes* the existence of a community. Any account of community which attempts to show it to be the product of agreement by pre-social individuals will turn out to be incoherent because such persons will turn out to lack the capacity to deliberate, to reflect, to choose. And Rawls's theory, Sandel maintains, bears this out. Its attempt to establish the terms of association (principles of justice) of a just society as the product of agreement among free and equal independent persons fails because such persons turn out to be formless ciphers without motivation or the capacity for reflection or choice. Such persons cannot reach substantive conclusions. To reach them Rawls is forced to invoke an assumption which is inconsistent with his theory: the assumption that there does already exist a community in whose life the individual is thoroughly implicated.

Sandel is also attacking Rawls's view that teleological theories which ask us to determine what is right by first establishing what is good are untenable. For Rawls, principles of right are established by the (hypothetical) choices of free and equal persons who accept the 'thin theory of the good', but do not themselves endorse any particular full theory of the good. Rawls's concern is that the selection of principles of right should not depend upon such contingent (and arbitrary) factors as prevailing desires or views of the good. Sandel's argument, however, is that the attempt to describe a standpoint from which a subject with only a thin conception of the good chooses right principles does not do the trick. Since choice for such an agent, at best, amounts to no more than identifying existing wants and matching them with the means of their satisfaction, prevailing desires and conceptions of the good will be thoroughly implicated in the selection of principles. Moreover, since the objects of reflection are arbitrarily-given desires undifferentiated as to worth, the principles chosen are not the product of serious examination of the good of various ways of life, or the worth of different orders of desires, but the result of the 'impoverished account of the good' common to utilitarianism as well as to justice as fairness (Sandel 1982, 167). Indeed, if the good is 'nothing more than the indiscriminate satisfaction of arbitrarily-given preferences, regardless of worth', and 'if conceptions of the good are morally arbitrary', Sandel observes, 'it becomes difficult to see why the highest of all (social) virtues should be the one that enables us to pursue the arbitrary conceptions "as fully as circumstances permit"' (Sandel 1982, 168).

If we are concerned, as Rawls claims to be, with our freedom, and wish to understand our agency as something more than the 'efficient administration' of our given desires and available means to their satisfaction, Sandel argues, then we must abandon Rawlsian liberalism and its understanding of our nature. We must see ourselves as capable of a more thoroughgoing reflection. And for this 'we cannot be wholly unencumbered subjects of possession, individuated in advance and given prior to our ends, but must be subjects constituted in part by our central aspirations and attachments, always open, indeed vulnerable, to growth and transformation in the light of revised self-understandings' (Sandel 1982, 172). Self-reflection, in this regard, means reflection upon ourselves, not merely as private, separate persons, but also as members of a community which shapes our identities by supplying 'a common vocabulary of discourse and a background of implicit practices and understandings' (Sandel 1982, 172–3). To reflect upon ourselves, and the nature of our good, would then be to reflect upon the good of the community.

Sandel thinks that all this intimates a quite different approach to moral philosophy. Our concern is not to stand back from our circumstances to try to judge our moral practices from some independent or impartial point of view. The end of moral reasoning is not judgment but understanding and self-discovery. I ask, not 'what should I be, what sort of life should I lead?', but 'who am I?' To ask this question is to concern oneself first and foremost with the character of the community which constitutes one's identity. It is to concern oneself with politics – the activity of attending to the demands of the community – rather than with such philosophical abstractions as justice.

Sandel's critique considered

Liberalism and the Limits of Justice has recently been described as 'the most thorough extended critique of Rawls's theory' (Arneson 1989, 695). But what is one to make of Sandel's challenge to Rawls? A fuller answer can only come after the arguments of his companion critics have been canvassed to provide a more complete picture of the communitarian challenge to Rawlsian liberalism. Yet some preliminary assessment may be in order.

For the most part, Sandel's account of Rawls's views is clear and accurate, and great credit is due to him for having provided a particularly penetrating analysis of the presuppositions of *A Theory of Justice*, and an important challenge to the political philosophy it represents. It is worthy of a fuller response than has been offered so far – by Rawls or his defenders. But the challenge is not without its flaws.

First, Sandel's critique of Rawls does not appear as damaging as he supposes. For Sandel, one of the weaknesses of Rawls's theory is that it presupposes the existence of a community whose values and concerns are implicit in the reasonings of the persons in the OP. So Rawls cannot properly claim that his principles of justice are the product of deliberation by independent agents without particular social commitments or values. Yet this is something Rawls has willingly conceded by the time Sandel comes to write his book. In his Dewey Lectures (1980) Rawls explicitly acknowledges that his concern is not to supply a universal standard of justice but to discover those moral principles which might best serve his own society, with all its particular concerns. The starting point of this philosophical inquiry is *not* the OP but the prevailing moral beliefs and intuitions of modern liberal democratic societies. Rawls proposes that we view that moral landscape *through* the OP, but makes it quite plain that the structure of the OP is designed to enable us to see more clearly what is presumed to be already there. We shall examine these changes in Rawls's thinking more closely in the next chapter. Sandel is not unfamiliar with the Dewey Lectures, for his book makes frequent reference to them. So it is puzzling that he overlooks or ignores the fact that there is another reading available which makes better sense of Rawls's work.

Secondly, it looks like an exaggeration to say that my social context *constitutes* my identity, however constitution is understood – we avoid this latter issue here. Quite clearly I can *identify* with my community; furthermore, I can *be identified* by my place within it. But this does not mean that my context defines who I am. Consider the case of Arthur, taken from his parents at birth by Merlin, and raised by a foster-father, not knowing he was heir to the throne. His social context identified him as the son of Ector and the brother of Kaye; he identified with his village and his home, not his kingdom. Yet his identity was that of King of the Britons. Even then, Arthur faced the problem of which 'identity' to choose, since his first inclination was to reject his inheritance in favour of the life he had known.

Indeed, it would seem that the self is, at best, only partly constituted by its context and its goals or ends, and is quite capable of participating in the determination of its identity. And Sandel admits as much when he concedes that persons are capable of more than just self-discovery. The 'subject' is empowered to participate in the constitution of its 'identity' (Sandel 1982, 152). It is able to make some choices about which of the 'possible purposes and ends all impinging indiscriminately on its identity' it will pursue, and which it will not (Sandel 1982, 152). But if these concessions are made, it becomes hard to see how Sandel's view of the self differs from Rawls's. As Kymlicka points out, the differences between Sandel's claims that the self is constituted by its ends, and that the boundaries of the self are fluid, and Rawls's view that the self is prior to its ends, and its boundaries are fixed antecedently, hide a more fundamental agreement. Both accept that the *person* is prior to his ends (Kymlicka 1988, 192). If Sandel allows that a self constituted by its ends can nonetheless be reconstituted, it is not clear how his view differs from that of the Rawlsian liberal. This is our third objection to Sandel.

Our fourth criticism is that Sandel never indicates why he thinks the self must be *politically* created. He may be right to suggest that the identity of the self is the product of experience, and cannot be taken for granted by a theory presuming that people exist with fully formed preferences and motives in some pre-social environment. But this does not mean that the self must be the product of *political* experience. To the extent that character is formed by the social environment, it is the family, the neighbourhood, and the local community that usually matter. These need not be, and typically are not, political communities. When political questions arise, they often do because of conflicts among these antecedently individuated communities and persons – among these already existing identities. Undoubtedly, many of those who grow up in any community will acquire political commitments. The liberal demand is that, in political *argument*, such commitments or attachments be left behind. If we all have such commitments, the fact of political commitment can carry no weight in any political dispute. Such commitments may lead us into politics, but they cannot deliver us from it. Taking such a view does not require us to embrace any implausible theses about personal identity or the nature of the self.

Finally, Sandel's contention that the end of moral reasoning is not judgment but understanding and self-discovery is, at best, implausible. Of course one can ask the question 'Who am I?' But self-discovery does not replace judgement about how to live one's life, or prevent one asking (or being asked): 'What should I be? What action should I take?' Often one must ask the first question to tackle the latter two. Before choosing to become a Christian, C. S Lewis was forced to examine his deeply-held atheistic beliefs. On Sandel's account he could have gone no further than the conclusion: 'I am an atheist' – or perhaps, on greater reflection: 'I am an English atheist'. Equally, we might regard someone who responded to a challenge to his actions with the reply, 'This is what I am' (or 'This is what we are'), as having failed to supply a moral argument, or indeed engage in the activity of moral reasoning.

Sandel's critique of Rawls's is powerful and important. But it is not decisive. While Rawls's arguments may rest on uncertain foundations, the presuppositions of Sandel's analysis are themselves open to question. Yet Sandel is only one of the communitarian objectors to Rawlsian liberalism. Do the others have nothing to say? Far from it, although for the most part they have developed their arguments not in response to Rawls alone. So let us turn to the communitarian critique more broadly conceived to see how it poses a challenge to Rawlsian liberalism.

THE COMMUNITARIAN CHALLENGE

We noted at the start that, for communitarians, thinkers like Rawls do not so much supply the wrong answers as pose the wrong questions. Thus Sandel accuses Rawls of focusing unduly on the question, 'What sort of life should I lead?' For communitarians, philosophers like Rawls are looking for the wrong thing: universal principles to serve as solutions to universal (or at least generalizable) problems – in this case, the problem of the nature of the best form of political association. The truth of the matter, however, is that there is no such problem except in the mind of the philosopher. The important problems arise *within* political associations. Their solutions are to be found using the resources afforded by the practices and traditions of enquiry which are central to the association. We do not look for universal principles – those abstractions created by philosophers – but turn inwards to try to discover the meanings implicit in our discourse and practice.

This position has been defended by Michael Walzer in his book *Spheres of Justice* (Walzer 1983) and, more importantly, in his article 'Philosophy and Democracy' (Walzer 1981). Walzer takes as his starting point Wittgenstein's statement: '"The philosopher is not a citizen of any community of ideas. That is what makes him into a philosopher"' (Walzer 1981, 393). The political philosopher is regarded as someone who has separated himself from the political community, 'cut himself loose from effective ties and conventional ideas' so that he can then 'ask and struggle to answer the deepest questions about the meaning and purpose of political association and the appropriate structure of the community (of every community) and its government' (Walzer 1981, 393). The philosopher is an outsider. Insiders, the members of the polity, however, ask different questions. They ask 'What is the meaning and purpose of *this* association? What is the appropriate structure of *our* community and government?' (Walzer 1981, 393). And if there are right answers to these latter questions, Walzer observes, there will be as many right answers as there are communities.

In the course of this argument Walzer alludes to one of Plato's most striking political analogies. In the *Republic* Plato asks us to imagine a dimly-lit cave inhabited by chained prisoners who mistake their fire-cast shadows for reality. The philosopher, for Plato, is the one who has broken free and acquired true knowledge in the clear sunlight of reason. His task is then to return to the cave to enlighten his fellows. Only he is truly fit to govern the good polity. For Walzer, however, the philosopher has no business in the cave, for his knowledge of universal truths can be of no relevance to the political community. The community asks political, not philosophical questions, and the answers it wants require political rather than philosophical knowledge. 'As there are many caves but only one sun, so political knowing is particular and pluralist in character, while philosophical knowing is universalist and singular' (Walzer 1981, 393). We must guard against the political success of philosophers because that would 'have the effect of enforcing a singular over a pluralist truth', and mean 'reiterating the structure of the ideal commonwealth in every particularist community' (Walzer 1981, 393). A dozen philosopher kings would fashion a dozen identical realms. And, in a clear reference to Rawls, Walzer notes: 'The case would be the same with a dozen communities founded in the original position: there is only one original position' (Walzer 1981, 393).

These sentiments are echoed by Michael Jackson, in his own critique of Rawls, when he writes that 'Cave dwellers have little to learn about the cave from philosophers of the sun' (Jackson 1986, 164). As cave dwellers, he observes, 'we know that our lives are ruled by political performance and not by philosophical promise', and this makes the 'search for transcultural criteria of justice . . . philosophically relevant, but . . . politically irrelevant' (Jackson 1986, 164).

This attitude lies at the heart of the communitarian hostility to Rawlsian liberalism. For communitarians, Rawls has asked that the practices of the community be examined in the cold light of the philosopher's reason, and evaluated against the abstract and unreal standards he has constructed and offered as principles. But to their mind Rawls has not offered a persuasive answer to the question he himself posed in *A Theory of Justice*: why should we take any interest, moral or otherwise, in the conclusions of the original position? These conclusions amount to nothing more than the imaginative constructions of the philosopher. To Walzer the philosopher is 'the only actual participant in the perfect meeting', and 'the principles, rules, constitutions, with which he emerges are in fact the products of his own thinking, "designed at will in an orderly fashion", subject only to whatever constraints he imposes on himself' (Walzer 1981, 389). And for Jackson Rawls's work, like all 'architectonic philosophy' is 'very definitely for card-carrying philosophers' (Jackson 1986, 168).

The task for those concerned with matters of justice, then, is not to look outward to abstract principles but to gaze inward, to discover the answers implicit in shared practices and traditions. Thus by Walzer's definition 'A given society is just if its substantive life is lived in a certain way – that is, in a way faithful to the shared understandings of the members' (Walzer 1983, 313). 'To override those understandings is (always) to act unjustly' (Walzer 1983, 314). As members of a society we can act or converse about justice only in the context of 'social meanings'. These meanings need not be 'harmonious': 'sometimes they provide only the intellectual structure within which distributions are debated' (Walzer 1983, 314). But the fact remains that there 'are no eternal or universal principles that can replace it. Every substantive account of distributive justice is a local account' (Walzer 1983, 314).

For Sandel we must look not to deontological principles of right, but to our own *common* good. Moral principles which are to have any hold upon us cannot be constructed in defiance of prevailing practices, and existing loyalties and obligations. To uncover such principles thus requires that we ask who we are, how we are situated, and what is to our good. This requires us also to ask what is good for the community, since we are 'partly defined by the communities we inhabit' and are therefore 'implicated in the purposes and ends characteristic of those communities' (Sandel 1988, 62). Sandel thus concurs wholeheartedly with Alasdair MacIntyre's view that 'what is good for me has to be the good for one who inhabits these roles' (MacIntyre 1986, 205). The story of my life is always embedded in the story of those communities from which I derive my identity (Sandel 1988, 62). Our concern should therefore be to ask, not 'What rights do I have?', but 'What is in our common good?'

A similar complaint is made by Charles Taylor who thinks that liberal theories, in giving priority to the individual's choice of ends, place individual rights above the claims of society. The unwarranted assumption of liberal thought, he argues, is that man can be regarded as self-sufficient, rational, and autonomous – independent of society. Liberalism conceives of man 'atomistically' and is, for this reason, unable to explain adequately the fact of human sociability. Because liberal institutions are founded on a mistaken account of man, those institutions themselves have an 'atomizing' effect on individuals. By focusing so much on individual 'rights', liberal institutions fail to consider the importance of sustaining the capacities that make individual choice possible. To do this, in Taylor's view, would require institutions that were concerned much more to ensure that the social context within which individuals operate was one that helps to nurture these capacities (Taylor 1985).

Like all the communitarians, Taylor thinks that we should pay more attention to the problem of how to sustain and preserve our traditions and communities, and less attention to the claims of individuals. This sentiment is echoed by MacIntyre, who argues that 'What matters at this stage is the construction of local forms of community within which civility and the intellectual and moral life can be sustained through the new dark ages which are already upon us' (MacIntyre 1986, 244). The demise of what he calls the 'tradition of the virtues' has led to our being governed not by any rational moral tradition but by a politics that amounts to little more than 'civil war carried on by other means' (MacIntyre 1986, 236): the barbarians no longer strain against our frontiers but 'have already been governing us for quite sometime' (MacIntyre 1986, 245). In *After Virtue* MacIntyre presents a philosophical history of Western moral theory which depicts the advent of Enlightenment liberalism as the crucial chapter in the demise of a rational moral tradition. In this time morality was transformed, fragmented and, ultimately, displaced. This period saw a 'change of belief' that was manifested, not only in the secularization of Protestantism, but also in a change in 'the modes of belief'. These social and philosophical changes raised key questions about the justification of moral belief. 'Morality' became 'the name for that particular sphere in which rules of conduct that were neither theological nor legal nor aesthetic are alllowed a cultural space of their own' (MacIntyre 1986, 38). With this development arose the project of finding an indepedent rational justification for morality – a project of which Rawls's theory of justice is our most famous recent example.

MacIntyre's argument is that this project of justifying morality broke down long ago. Moreover, our modern predicament is that we continue to engage in this hopeless undertaking. It is in his view implausible to expect that social arrangements be assessed from some disinterested, impartial, external point of view and still hope that they be judged by standards that have genuine moral worth. 'Only within a community with shared beliefs about goods, and shared dispositions educated in accordance with those beliefs, both rooted in shared practices, can practical reason-giving be an ordered, teachable activity with standards of success and failure' (MacIntyre 1983, 591). Modern liberals like Rawls, however, are contributing nothing towards the task of reconstruction of community but persist in a project that is foredoomed to failure. This is why modern life exhibits such terrible intellectual and social dissensus.

Are the communitarians right? We think not. And while there is not space here to offer the fuller response the communitarian philosophies warrant, it is worth indicating where they go astray – particularly in their assessment of Rawls. (A 1989 *Ethics* symposium on Rawls contains a number of papers which assess and respond to the communitarian challenge. See in particular Doppelt 1989, Allen Buchanan 1989 and Kymlicka 1989.)

Our first criticism of the communitarians is that they have misinterpreted Rawls in assuming that he is looking to construct the good society from scratch, or discover universal moral principles without reference to the moral practices of existing societies. Yet as we noted in our consideration of Sandel, Rawls has quite explicitly stated that his starting point is the moral practices of his own society. The question is, what should those moral practices be, given the background of intuitions and commitments in our society. The original position is a device which offers us a way of theorizing about this issue. As we noted in chapters 3 and 4, the OP cannot be the starting point of moral inquiry; Rawls argues *through* the OP to establish his conclusions. So when Sandel and Walzer argue that we should turn to reflect upon the meanings and understandings implicit in our existing moral practices, they cannot complain that Rawls is doing otherwise.

There is, however, the quite different criticism that the *method* Rawls has adopted of investigating the principles underlying our moral and political practices is inadequate. Rawls the philosopher is staying within the community, but he is nonetheless judging it by standards which are foreign – which come from beyond the cave. Rawls is a modern-day gadfly whose reasonings are at worst disruptive and at best irrelevant. The truth is that in the polity decisions are taken through political (and for Walzer, democratic) and not philosophical processes. In Rawls's argument justice is divorced from politics. 'The divide between politics and justice is nowhere more plain to see than in Rawls's approach to justice', remarks Michael Jackson; and 'if politics and justice are antithetical, then justice will never be done' (Jackson 1986, 156).

Yet there is surely some point in what Rawls has done. His starting point, after all, is the existence of politics or, more precisely, political disagreement. The question then is, how do we resolve the disagreements that make for competing political claims? 'Politics' is not an adequate answer, for the question is raised *within* the context of politics. We need to step out of its hurly-burly if we think we ought to try to find good reasons for our actions (and if we assume that 'it is in my interest' is not *always* a good reason). We are, as Kant said, 'impelled to go outside its sphere in order to escape from the perplexity of opposing claims' (quoted in Kymlicka 1988a, 201). And this leads us to philosophy.

Now this does, of course, mean distinguishing philosophy from politics. But could it be otherwise? A philosophical argument which papered over its weaknesses with appeals to political considerations could hardly be *philosophically* persuasive. Undoubtedly such moves are made all the time in politics – and only the most naive optimist would expect this ever to change – since politics is the art of the possible and not reflection upon the desirable. But there must be some place in political life for such reflection. All the more so if we are to take our politics seriously.

Of course a philosophical argument which *relied* on implausible assumptions about the nature of political life would be a poor one. But Rawls does give consideration to the question of the *feasibility* of his principles of justice, whether or not his approach to the feasibility question is adequate.

Finally, while the communitarians have been persistently critical of Rawls and the political philosophy of liberalism, they leave themselves open to the counter-question: 'How would *you* theorize about politics?' This retort has some point not because the critic is obliged always to have some alternative up his sleeve. It has point because it is often hard to see how the communitarian critics of liberalism intend to distinguish their substantive views from those they try to criticize.

Sandel, for example, as we noted earlier, criticizes Rawls for failing to offer an account of the self as constituted by its communal attachments. Yet, as Gutmann has pointed out, Sandel himself suggests that 'community is "a mode of self-understanding *partly* constitutive" of our identity' (Gutmann 1985, 317). If the self is only partly constituted by the community, how does this distinguish Sandel's from the liberal view? (Kymlicka makes the same point in 1988, 192).

Similarly MacIntyre, in his criticism of the liberal failure to provide a substantive account of the human good, arrives at this 'provisional conclusion' about the good life: 'the good life for man is the life spent in seeking for the good life for man, and the virtues necessary for the seeking are those which will enable us to understand what more and what else the good life for man is' (MacIntyre 1986, 204). Yet this conclusion, particularly in its provisionality, is not so far from the liberal insistence that the good society is one in which individuals are left free to discover what is the good life.

Here the communitarians would object that we neglect two crucial points. First, they insist that the good life, while it may vary with person and place, is dependent upon one's 'social identity' (MacIntyre 1986, 204): 'what is good for me has to be the good for one who inhabits these roles' (MacIntyre 1986, 205). Secondly, they say that I inherit from the past of my family, tribe and nation a variety of debts, inheritances and obligations which 'constitute the given of my life, my moral starting point' (MacIntyre 1986, 205).

The first objection is not a strong one. As Gutmann tellingly asks, 'What follows from "what is good for me has to be the good for someone who was born female into a first-generation American, working-class Italian, Catholic family?"' (Gutmann 1985, 316). The fact remains that the good life for me does not depend *wholly* on my social identity. As for the second objection, it remains to be discovered *how* the different claims I have and have made upon me by my history are to be ordered and reconciled.

It is difficult to identify the differences between liberals and communitarians on many points that the latter find of critical interest. At times the communitarians seem like sheep in wolves' clothing. Nonetheless the communitarian critique has been an influential one. And if at times there seem to be fewer differences between them and Rawls than one might be led to expect, it is at least an open question as to how much this is the result of Rawls's thought moving in a more communitarian direction. This is a topic we shall turn to presently.

SUMMARY

The communitarian critique of Rawls, we have tried to show, is one which poses a fundamental challenge to the liberal approach to political philosophy. It identifies in Rawls's theory of justice weaknesses it considers to be characteristic of liberal theory in general. For Sandel, the characteristic weakness is to be found in the incoherences associated with the notion of the self presupposed by Rawls's theory of justice. For the communitarians generally, it lies in the implausibility of the idea that there are universal standards by which the practices of particular communities may sensibly be judged. Against the communitarians we have suggested that their critique falls short of its target inasmuch as they have either misunderstood Rawls, or relied on presuppositions as contentious as those underlying *A Theory of Justice*, or themselves embraced views which make them not so different from the liberals they attack.

7

The Self-Critique

Rawls has not been idle since *A Theory of Justice* first appeared. The past two decades have seen him publish a series of articles elaborating points of his theory, defending others against objections and misunderstandings, and, to some extent, modifying or re-interpreting his own work to accommodate criticisms. These writings include the Dewey Lectures on 'Kantian Constructivism in Moral Theory' (Rawls 1980), the Tanner Lectures on 'The Basic Liberties and Their Priority' (1982a), and four recent articles dealing with the nature of his enterprise (1985, 1987, 1988 and 1989), as well as various papers elaborating on the maximin criterion (1974), primary goods (Rawls 1982b) and the 'basic structure as subject' (1978).

The obvious question to ask is: has his thinking changed? That is what we turn to now. To supply a meaningful answer, however, will require more than a summary of the replies and the elaborations Rawls has offered in recent years. All of these writings have attempted to strengthen and defend the elements of a political philosophy he has held to for some time. We need, therefore, to be able to distinguish shifts of emphasis from changes of greater substance (or to see when shifts of emphasis are so marked as to constitute changes of substance). Our hope is that this will not only lead to an understanding of Rawls's current thinking, but also offer us some critical insight into the nature of his thought, and its place in modern political philosophy.

To attempt the task of accounting for the the development of Rawls's thought is hazardous. Mere exposition of a thinker's work can be contentious enough, since all such exercises require interpretation. An attempt to follow his intellectual movements is doubly difficult because it involves making claims about the relative significance of the various elements in his thought – claims which the thinker himself may find surprising, and even mistaken. Nonetheless, we shall try to offer an account of the development of Rawls's thought, fully recognizing that we are presenting an interpretation which may prove more contentious than anything we have said so far.

The thesis we will advance is that Rawls's writings since 1971 reveal two important movements. The first movement takes us as far as 1982 when the Tanner Lectures on 'The Basic Liberties and Their Priority' were published. In this period Rawls also published two other works of especial importance: 'The Basic Structure as Subject' (1978) and the Dewey Lectures on 'Kantian Constructivism in Moral Theory' (1980). In these works, we suggest, Rawls offers a series of replies to objections, along with some changes to and elaborations of his theory of justice, which go to provide a deeper understanding of the Kantian nature of his moral philosophy.

The second movement takes us, roughly, from 1982 onwards. Rawls's three most important papers here are 'Justice as Fairness: Political not Metaphysical' (1985), 'The Idea of an Overlapping Consensus' (1987), and 'The Priority of Right and Ideas of the Good' (1988). In this period Rawls forswears Kantianism and recasts his philosophical enterprise as a political rather than a moral endeavour.

As we shall see after an examination of these two movements, the development of Rawls's thought in the seventies and eighties brings him to a new, and in our view highly questionable, view of the nature and the role of political philosophy. One point needs to be made before turning to the account of the changes in Rawls's thought. In distinguishing two 'movements' we do not intend to suggest that there is any decisive break in Rawls's thinking: themes which dominate his later papers are also to be found in the Dewey Lectures, for example. The point of identifying distinct periods is to provide some sense of the *development* of Rawls's thinking.[1]

THE FIRST MOVEMENT: RAWLS 1971–82

Rawls's earliest critics were quick to note two features of his theory of justice. First, they said, he has provided not so much a universal theory of justice as a rationalization of some modern beliefs. Steven Lukes, for example, in a review in the *Observer* in 1972, suggested that the conclusions of the parties in the Original Position were unsurprising only because 'the motivation, beliefs and indeed the very rationality of Rawls's "individuals" are recognizably those of some modern, Western, liberal, individualistic men' (Lukes 1978, 189). And similar points were made by Philip Pettit (1974), David Miller (1976), and Milton Fisk (1978), to name just a handful of commentators.

Secondly, they noted that Rawls's theory was contractarian theory with particular affinities with Kant's moral philosophy. Philosophers such as Robert Paul Wolff thus argued that Rawls's theory bore many of the weaknesses of Kant's endeavour to 'deduce objective, obligatory ends from the mere analysis of what it is to be a rational agent' (Wolff 1977, 111). Wolff's judgement is worth quoting fully.

> The heart of Rawls's philosophy is the idea of the bargaining game, by means of which the sterility of Kant's formal reasoning was to be overcome, and a principle was to be established that would combine the strengths and avoid the weaknesses of utilitarianism and intuitionism. The idea is original, powerful, and elegant, but it simply does not stand

> up. The original sketch of the bargaining game was comprehensible, but it was open to crushing objections. The device of the veil of ignorance enables Rawls at least initially to avoid the pitfalls of the first model while seeming to link his philosophy to that of Kant. But the move is ultimately fatal, for in striving for absolute universality, for a contemplation of the foundations of social philosophy *sub specie aeternitatis*, Rawls abstracts from all that is characteristically human and social. The result is a model of a choice problem that is not sufficiently determined to admit of solution, and neither historical nor human enough to bear a useful relationship to the real issues of social theory. (Wolff 1977, 179)

In response to these two criticisms, Rawls began to fashion a reply which at once admitted that his theory was better understood as a philosophy for modern liberal democratic polities, and yet maintained that the modified Kantian structure of his argument was not undermined by the traditional objections to Kant, and to social contract theory more generally.

In making the first admission, Rawls takes great pains to show that his theory was never vulnerable to the charge that it presupposes an asocial conception of the individual. This conception Rawls defines as the doctrine that 'the fundamental aims and interests of individuals are determined independently from particular social forms; society and the state are regarded as institutional arrangements that answer to these antecedent individual ends and purposes, as specified by a fixed and invariant human psychology' (1975, 547). The interests of individuals, in his theory, he argued in 'Fairness to Goodness', 'depend upon existing institutions and the principles of justice they satisfy' (1975, 547). Writers like Lukes are thus mistaken to suggest that *A Theory of Justice* relies on an asocial conception of people (see Lukes 1973, 75, 139).

This point is emphasized in a number of Rawls's papers, including 'The Basic Structure as Subject' (1978) and 'A Well-Ordered Society' (1979 – first published in 1975 as 'A Kantian Conception of Equality'), where Rawls tries to make clear that, while justice as fairness has 'a suitably individualistic base', it 'can accommodate the social nature of human beings' (1978, 67). In his view 'the two principles of justice regulate how entitlements are acquired in return for contributions to associations, or to other forms of cooperation, within the basic structure' (1978, 62). In seeking principles of regulation, the worth of society itself is never in question; the issue of the appropriate form of regulation is raised within a society in which the various associations already exist. And the parties to the contract that establishes the principles 'are described in terms that have an institutional expression' (1978, 63), which means that they are assumed to be social – as they are not in classical utilitarianism which takes as basic only the capacity for pleasure and pain.

So what is (and has always been) at issue for Rawls is 'background justice' in already existing societies. By the time he came to present the Dewey Lectures, however, Rawls was clear that his focus was more parochial still. Now he maintained that his concern in developing a Kantian conception of justice was to address 'an impasse in our recent political history', evident in the absence of agreement over the past two centuries of American history 'on the way basic social institutions should be arranged if they are to conform to the freedom and equality of citizens as moral persons' (1980, 517). In these lectures Rawls is unequivocal: his concern is to find, not universal principles of justice, but principles appropriate for modern societies like the United States.

> An immediate consequence of taking our inquiry as focussed on the apparent conflict between freedom and equality in a democratic society is that we are not trying to find a conception of justice suitable for all societies regardless of their particular social or historical circumstances. We want to settle a fundamental disagreement over the just form of basic institutions within a democratic society under modern conditions. We look to ourselves and to our future, and reflect

> upon our disputes since, let's say, the Declaration of Independence. How far the conclusions we reach are of interest in a wider context is a separate question. (1980, 518; see also 1982, 84–5)

It is important to note how emphatic Rawls is that his solution to this problem is to develop a *Kantian* conception of justice. Quite clearly he believes that the criticisms of his theory coming from Hegelian or communitarian quarters can be accommodated without abandoning the Kantian structure of his argument. Indeed, in the Dewey Lectures, he suggests that one of his aims is to overcome the dualisms in Kant's doctrine so strongly criticized by Hegel (1980, 516). And while he is quick to add that justice as fairness is not Kant's view strictly speaking, and that 'the adjective "Kantian" expresses analogy and not identity', he leaves no doubt that his doctrine 'sufficiently resembles Kant's in enough fundamental respects so that it is far closer to his view than to the other traditional moral conceptions that are appropriate for use as benchmarks of comparison' (1980, 517). The question for us is, how does this modified Kantianism serve Rawls's purposes? To find the answer we shall have to look more closely at Rawls's re-interpretation of his own theory.

The aim of political philosophy, he now suggests, is to articulate and make explicit the shared notions latent in common sense, or, if common sense is uncertain, 'to propose to it certain conceptions and principles congenial to its most essential convictions and historical traditions' (Rawls 1980, 518). So what is required is not merely correct reasoning from correct, or even publicly shared premises: 'The real task is to *discover* and *formulate* the deeper bases of agreement which one hopes are embedded in common sense, or even to originate and fashion starting points for common understanding' (1980, 518 italics added).

Clearly, Rawls is still interested in discovering principles of justice. But now he says he is also looking to 'formulate' the bases of agreement, or to 'originate and fashion' starting points for common understanding. As the title of his Dewey Lectures suggest, he is now looking also to *construct* a conception of justice. His concern is not only with using the device of hypothetical agreement to uncover moral principles, but to 'search for reasonable grounds for reaching agreement' (1980, 519). His task, as he now conceives it, is as much 'to articulate a public conception of justice that all can live with who regard their person and their relation to society in a certain way' (1980, 519). On the one hand imagining what we would agree to (in idealized conditions) will reveal to us the right principles of justice; on the other hand, we need to construct such principles as will secure agreement.

What Rawls says now is quite consistent with his avowed concerns in *A Theory of Justice*. He still thinks that it is 'perfectly proper' that 'argument for the principles of justice proceed from some consensus' (581). But he now concedes that this consensus has to be that which is found not in universal society but in a more restricted group. The contract defines or helps us to formulate what is just – for us. We can still think of the contract as a heuristic device, but what it identifies is not 'justice', only 'what is just for us'. In particular, it determines whether the Kantian conception of justice as fairness is right for us.

The approach that Rawls recommends he describes as 'Kantian constructivism'. It is constructivist because we are directed in the first place to the construction of a fair procedure, the idea being that if the procedure is fair, the outcome will be fair: this is pure procedural justice. The approach is Kantian because Rawls, like Kant, wants to supply justifications for moral principles which are not dependent for their legitimacy on the vagaries of human nature – on human desires, passions or instincts. Kantian constructivism is an attempt to do this.

The important move in this attempt is in Rawls's claim that the content of a conception of justice is determined, not by some account of human behaviour, but by a 'conception of the person'. He takes the question to be, how can people settle on a conception of justice 'that is (most) reasonable for them *in virtue of how they conceive of their persons* and construe the general features of social cooperation among persons so regarded' (1980, 517, emphasis added)? This is, more specifically, a question addressed to American society which, on Rawls's reading of its political history, conceives of moral persons as 'free and equal', but enjoys 'no agreement about the way basic social institutions should be arranged to conform to the freedom and equality of citizens as moral persons' (1980, 517). What is needed is a theory which supplies right principles for this society through a consideration of the conception of the person, and the ideal of the good society, implicit in its common life.

This approach differs from that taken by the mainstream of classical theorists of the American polity such as James Madison and John C. Calhoun, who begin with accounts of (self-interested) human nature, and regard political institutions as mechanisms designed to minimize the evils that result when individuals pursue private gain – whether through the market or through politics. Their views owed much to David Hume's theories of human nature and politics. Rawls, however, looks to Kant; human nature plays no part in the presuppositions of his argument. His aim is not to find principles that would be of instrumental value (in governing the institutions which curb our excesses) but to find a conception of justice which would itself command allegiance because expressive of our moral personhood. He differs from Kant largely in his concession that moral personhood is not a universal property but varies from one moral tradition to another.

How, then, does Rawls go about the task of finding 'a suitable rendering of freedom and equality, and of their relative priority, rooted in the more fundamental notions of our political life and congenial to our conception of the person' (1980, 520)? In his own account of his method, he suggests that justice as fairness tries to uncover the latent ideas of freedom and equality, of ideal social cooperation, and of the person, by 'formulating' two 'model-conceptions', one of a '*well-ordered society*' and another of a '*moral person*'. These model-conceptions 'single out the essential aspects of our conception of ourselves as moral persons and of our relation to society as free and equal citizens', and 'depict certain general features of what a society would look like if its members publicly viewed themselves and their social ties with one another in a certain way' (1980, 520).

The *original position* is a third, 'mediating model-conception' whose role is to 'establish the connection between the model-conception of a moral person and the principles of justice that characterize the relations of citizens in the model-conception of a well-ordered society' (1980, 520). It does this by modelling the way in which citizens in a well-ordered society, viewed as moral persons, would ideally select principles of justice. The constraints imposed on the parties in the OP help to represent them as free and equal moral persons; and if certain principles of justice would be agreed to then Kantian constructivism succeeds in connecting definite principles with a particular conception of the person.

What is the conception of a well-ordered society implicit in the American tradition? Rawls suggests that it is, first, a society 'effectively regulated by a public conception of justice' (1980, 521). Secondly, it is one in which its members are, and view themselves and one another in their political and social relations (as far as justice is concerned) as, free and equal moral persons. And thirdly, it is stable inasmuch as it is governed by a stable sense of justice. (Rawls offers a fuller account of the nature of the well-ordered society in the second Dewey Lecture.)

What is the conception of the person implicit in the American tradition? Moral persons in this society, according to Rawls, are characterized by two moral powers and two corresponding 'highest-order interests' (1980, 525). Moral persons have the power or capacity for an effective sense of justice, and the power to form, revise and rationally pursue a conception of the good. Corresponding to these moral powers, they are moved by two highest-order interests in realizing and exercising these powers. They also have a third, 'higher-order interest in protecting and advancing their conception of the good as best they can' (1980, 525).

The original position, then, is a device which serves to draw out the principles of justice appropriate for a polity which (implicitly) holds to these models of the person and of the well-ordered society. It does this because it is constructed and peopled in a way which reflects the values implicit in the two model conceptions of the person and the well-ordered society. Thus the OP brings down a 'veil of ignorance' to ensure that reasoning cannot be influenced by inequalities of wealth, status or talent, and the persons are taken to have a preference for 'primary goods' because these are the goods that are necessary 'as social conditions and all-purpose means to enable human beings to realize and exercise their moral powers and to pursue their final ends' (1980, 526).[2] When various conceptions of justice are tested, one against another, in the OP, justice as fairness comes up trumps as the conception that is chosen by these people, in conditions modelled to favour the values of modern liberal democratic societies like America.

So while each person in the OP simply asks 'what principles would it be rational for me to accept?', the answer that all concur with is not really an answer to an *abstract* question about what conception of justice it would be rational to adopt. The question has a context. And that context is society; or at least, society as it has been modelled in the OP. This context or framework within which rational choice takes place Rawls characterizes as 'the *Reasonable*'. At its heart lies a notion of the '*fair terms of cooperation*' which all rational choosers in this society accept. This notion expresses an idea of 'reciprocity and mutuality: all who cooperate must benefit, or share in common burdens, in some appropriate fashion as judged by a suitable benchmark of comparison' (1980, 528). The Reasonable, Rawls says, is 'incorporated into the background setup of the original position which frames the discussions of the parties and situates them symmetrically' (1980, 529). It is a demand of the Reasonable that, in addition to various familiar formal conditions on first principles, such as generality and universality, the parties are required to adopt a public conception of justice and must assess first principles with this condition in mind (1980, 529). The Reasonable, in other words, supports the demands associated with what figure in *A Theory of Justice* as constraints of the concept of right.

But social cooperation involves attempting to advance one's own good as well as recognizing the fair terms of cooperation associated with the Reasonable. Rawls refers to this aspect of cooperation as 'the *Rational*'. In the OP the Rational is interpreted in terms of persons' desires to realize and to exercise their moral powers and to advance their conceptions of the good. But always this is constrained by the Reasonable. The relationship between the Reasonable and the Rational is of crucial importance, for Rawls is at pains to maintain that he is not deriving his conclusions from some abstract conception of rationality. This is why he emphasizes that 'the Reasonable presupposes and subordinates the Rational' (1980, 530).

The Reasonable presupposes the Rational, because, without conceptions of the good that move members of the group, there is no point to social cooperation nor to notions of right and justice, even though such cooperation realizes values that go beyond what conceptions of the good specify taken alone. The Reasonable subordinates the Rational because its principles limit, and in a Kantian doctrine limit absolutely, the final ends that can be pursued (1980, 530).

This is a point of great importance in trying to understand Rawls's kind of Kantianism, because it suggests that critics such as Wolff can no longer accuse him of 'striving for absolute universality', or of an approach that 'abstracts from all that is characteristically human and social' (Wolff 1977, 179). Rawls's starting point is a particular (liberal democratic American) social conception of what is reasonable which *subordinates* considerations of rationality.

The nature and point of this distinction between the Reasonable and the Rational is brought out most clearly in the Tanner Lectures. These lectures were conceived as a response to criticisms raised by H. L. A. Hart against the account of liberty offered in *A Theory of Justice*. Hart observed that Rawls had failed to explain adequately why the parties in the OP would adopt the basic liberties and accept their priority, and had also failed to explain how the basic liberties were to be further specified in the light of particular social conditions (Hart 1978). In Rawls's theory, once the principles of justice were chosen in the OP, there follow three further stages of implementation, as the parties move to a constitutional convention establishing the rights of citizens, then to a legislative stage where the justice of laws and policies are considered, and finally to the stage of judicial interpretation of particular cases. Hart's point was that it was not clear how the principles of justice could be of much use in this process in which, presumably, the doctrine acquired greater substantive content.

Rawls's first response was to revise the first principle. (It now reads: 'Each person has an equal right to a fully adequate scheme of equal basic liberties which is compatible with a similar scheme of liberties for all' (1982a, 5). Rawls says that he now assigns no priority to 'liberty as such', but only to certain basic liberties. Hart had rightly pointed out an ambiguity in *A Theory of Justice* in which Rawls defended specific 'basic liberties' and yet maintained a principle of 'greatest equal liberty' in more general terms (holding that liberty could only be restricted for the sake of liberty). A coherent interpretation of Rawls's book, Hart noted, suggested that he meant only to defend the basic liberties (Hart 1978, 236). Rawls concurred. He did not wish to defend the priority of liberty as such, but certain basic liberties. 'Throughout the history of democratic thought the focus has been on achieving certain specific liberties and constitutional guarantees, as found, for example, in various bills of rights and declarations of the rights of man. The account of the basic liberties follows this tradition' (1982a, 6). The list of liberties was to be considered as one to be specified further at the constitutional, legislative, and judicial stages

(1982a, 7).[3] As Rawls now explains it, at each of these four stages, beginning in the OP, 'the Reasonable frames and subordinates the Rational', although the task of the rational agents, and the constraints they work under, vary (1982a, 55). Thus the parties in the OP are constrained by conditions of reasonableness when they choose principles of the basic structure; delegates to a constitutional convention apply these principles to select a constitution; and legislators make laws that must accord with the constitution and basic principles. At each successive stage the agents have less leeway as they are more and more constrained by the conclusions of previous stages. They have to act rationally, but as the task becomes less general and more specific, the demands of the Reasonable become stronger (and the veil of ignorance becomes thinner) (1982, 55). 'While the constraints of the Reasonable are weakest and the veil of ignorance thickest in the original position, at the judicial stage these constraints are strongest and the veil of ignorance thinnest' (1982, 55).

In developing this argument much of Rawls's energy is directed at one goal: to show that the elaboration of a Kantian conception of justice is not a matter of conjuring up abstractions. He is engaged in the practical task of seeking a way to bridge the impasse in American political culture that exists because of disagreements over the import of the ideals of freedom and equality. His solution is a Kantian conception of justice which, he thinks, can be embraced because it is consistent with the conception of the person and the ideal of the well-ordered society implicit in an American tradition which gives pride of place to freedom and equality.

Rawls's most important writings from 1975 up to 1982, and particularly the Dewey Lectures, stress the Kantian nature of this enterprise. Indeed, the final theory is presented as something of an improvement upon Kant's moral philosophy in many respects. It is, for example, not open to the criticisms made of Kant that the maxims of his categorical imperative were, ultimately, tested by their tendency to fulfil man's natural inclinations and needs. Rawls's theory does not rest on any view of human nature, or conceive of the demands of morality as conditional in this way. 'In justice as fairness, the Reasonable frames the Rational and is derived from a conception of moral persons as free and equal. Once this is understood, the constraints of the original position are no longer external' (1980, 532).

Moreover, the way in which the Reasonable frames the Rational in the OP, according to Rawls, 'represents a feature of the unity of practical reason' (1980, 532). In Kant's terms, empirical practical reason is represented by the rational deliberations of the parties; pure practical reason is represented by the constraints within which these deliberations take place. The unity of practical reason is expressed by defining the Reasonable to frame the Rational and to subordinate it absolutely; that is, the principles of justice that are agreed to are lexically prior in their application in a well-ordered society to claims of the good (1980, 532).

But perhaps most important is the fact that the ideal Rawls adheres to is the Kantian ideal of autonomy. A well-ordered society is conceived of as one peopled by autonomous citizens. It is this autonomy the OP models when the parties therein are conceived as rationally autonomous. When we act according to the principles such persons would choose under Reasonable conditions, we enjoy the sort of autonomy Kant held up as the highest moral ideal.

In effect, the first movement of Rawls's later thought suggests that he is able to resolve two major problems. The first is the problem of the reconciliation of the demands of freedom with the demands of equality as expressed in the conflict in American political culture between its Lockean and Rousseauesque inheritances. Its solution is presented in the articulation of a Kantian conception of justice. The second is the problem of the abstractness of Kant's moral doctrine. This is resolved by the development of the theory of the original position as the framework of reasonableness which constrains, and ultimately yields the substantive content of, rational reflection.

The boldness and ambition of these philosophical claims is quite breathtaking. It makes it all the more startling to find that, within a short time, Rawls moves away from the Kantian interpretation of his conception of justice to put an altogether different gloss on the theory.

THE SECOND MOVEMENT: RAWLS 1982–1989

The first movement of Rawls's later thought, as we have seen, may be viewed as a response to the charge that he was dealing in abstractions. Rawls tried to show that this charge was false by arguing that he had developed a Kantian moral philosophy rooted securely in an understanding of the deepest values of the liberal democratic culture of America. He had developed a moral philosophy we might describe as 'Kantianism in one country'.

The second movement, we wish to suggest, responds to quite different criticisms of Rawls's thinking. These criticisms come primarily from the communitarians. The objection which Rawls concerns himself with is the charge that his theory depends on particular metaphysical claims about the essential nature and identity of persons, and involves certain philosophical claims to universal truth. Rawls wishes to deny these charges; but the process of denial takes his thought down new – and controversial – paths.

In some ways it is surprising that Rawls should feel the need to deal with such charges. We noted in the previous chapter that communitarians like Sandel had, quite inexplicably, dealt with Rawls's theory of justice without taking adequate notice of his later writings, and particularly of the changes made in the Dewey Lectures. It is odd that Sandel in particular, who develops the most sophisticated case for viewing Rawls as committed to untenable metaphysical theses about the nature of the self, should have failed to consider the arguments advanced by Rawls in his 1974 Presidential Address to the American Philosophical Association, entitled 'The Independence of Moral Theory' (1974–5). Here Rawls defended the view that moral philosophy was not dependent upon the conclusions of other branches of philosophy, including the philosophy of mind, with its concerns with the problem of personal identity (1974–5, 15–20).

It is also surprising that so few of Rawls's critics have taken serious notice of Rawls's insistence in all his works, beginning with his 'Outline of a Decision Procedure for Ethics' (1951), that his starting point is the problem of finding reasonable solutions to conflicts within existing practice. He is looking for a way of adjudicating between the competing claims of different interests (1951, 177). Justice requires 'the establishment, *within the structure of a practice*, of a proper balance between competing claims (1957, 653 emphases added). To discover what principles of justice would be reasonable does not require appeal to other philosophical conclusions, but calls for some method or procedure for identifying reasonable solutions. Ethical conclusions were not to be *deduced* from other philosophical premises. Ethics was more like an inductive enterprise than a deductive one (1951, 178).

Nonetheless, in responding to critics who accuse him of seeking to deduce universal principles from abstract premises committed to a particular view of human nature, Rawls does not simply return to the claims of his earliest writings. His enterprise is now conceived somewhat differently, and he is concerned to emphasize different things, though, as we shall see, important continuities remain.

What Rawls now emphasizes is that his theory of justice is best understood as a *political* rather than as a moral doctrine – and as such is committed to no metaphysical theses. Justice as fairness, he says, 'is intended as a political conception of justice' (1985, 224). Thus his Dewey Lectures on 'Kantian Constructivism in Moral Theory' he now thinks would have been better titled 'Kantian Constructivism in Political Philosophy' (1985, 224n.). Rawls draws a new distinction which is basic to his discussions: a distinction 'between a political conception of justice and a *comprehensive* religious, philosophical, or moral doctrine' (1988, 252 emphasis added).

What he seeks to provide is a public philosophy which does not incorporate or amount to any comprehensive doctrine.

Let us look more closely at this distinction before turning to Rawls's reasons for making it. There are, he says, three distinguishing features of a *political* conception of justice. First, it is 'a moral conception worked out for a specific subject, namely, the basic structure of a constitutional democratic regime' (1988, 252). Secondly, accepting a political conception does not require accepting any particular religious, philosophical or moral doctrine: 'the political conception presents itself as a reasonable conception for the basic structure alone' (1988, 252). Thirdly, 'it is formulated not in terms of any comprehensive doctrine but in terms of certain fundamental intuitive ideas viewed as latent in the public political culture of a democratic society' (1988, 252). The difference between political and other conceptions is largely one of 'scope'. Comprehensive conceptions involve accounts of what is of value in human life and ideals of personal virtue and character which are to govern all parts of one's life, and not just the political. A fully comprehensive doctrine covers all recognized values and virtues within a precisely articulated scheme of thought. A 'partially comprehensive' doctrine is one which comprises some, but not all, nonpolitical values and virtues in a loosely articulated scheme (1988, 253).

Rawls is led to develop this distinction because of the way in which he now conceives of the task of political philosophy – and of his own political philosophy in particular – and because of his conclusions about what is necessary if this task is to be completed. As he first suggested in the Dewey Lectures, he is looking to deal with certain problems which have led to an impasse in American political history. There is a conflict among various understandings of the ideals of freedom and equality which reflect the different strands of America's philosophical inheritance.

But this conflict is not merely academic. It involves modern society as a whole, a society about which four 'general facts of political sociology and human psychology'

(1989, 234) are of crucial importance. First, it is a permanent feature of the public cultures of modern democratic societies such as America that they harbour a diversity of moral, religious, intellectual and philosophical doctrines, which hold to a plurality of conflicting, or even incommensurable, conceptions of the meaning, value and purpose of life. Second, 'only the oppressive use of state power can maintain a continuing common affirmation of one comprehensive religious, philosophical, or moral doctrine' (1989, 35). Third, an enduring and secure democratic regime must be willingly and freely supported by at least a substantial majority of its politically active citizens. And fourth, 'the political culture of a reasonably stable democratic society normally contains, at least implicitly, certain fundamental intuitive ideas from which it is possible to work up a political conception of justice suitable for a constitutional regime' (1989, 35). The task of political philosophy in such societies is to find a solution to the problem of how to ensure stability and social unity.

> In a constitutional democracy one of its most important aims is presenting a political conception of justice that can not only provide a shared public basis for the justification of political and social institutions but also helps ensure stability from one generation to the next. (1987, 1)

This is an important task. Since the diversity of doctrines – the fact of pluralism – is not a mere historical condition that will soon pass away but 'a permanent feature of the public culture of modern democracies' (1987, 4), stability and social unity are threatened insofar as unresolved disagreements may perpetuate and intensify the deep divisions latent in society, thereby increasing the insecurity and hostility of public life. The danger is that, in such a condition, groups or sections of society would be only too ready to pursue their more parochial interests whenever the opportunity arises. With this the possibility of social cooperation under a stable social unity diminishes.

How does political philosophy help to secure stability, and ensure that we will see 'social unity sustained in long-run equilibrium'? For Rawls, it does this by finding a conception of justice which will allow the members of society to examine before one another whether or not their political institutions are just. 'It enables them to do this by citing what are recognized among them as valid and sufficient reasons singled out by that conception itself' (1987, 6).

Now, if this is how political philosophy is to fulfil its task, two ways of proceeding have to be eliminated. First, political philosophy cannot proceed by looking for principles of constitutional design to guide the construction of political institutions which would moderate the harmful influence of self- or group-interests. The paths taken by Madison and Calhoun, to Rawls's way of thinking, must be abandoned. A polity which depended for its stability on institutions created to keep contending interests (or human nature) in check would be 'a mere *modus vivendi*, dependent on a fortuitous conjunction of contingencies' (1987, 1). The stability Rawls is looking to secure must take the form of a deeper social unity which would not collapse under the pressure of changed circumstances or shifts in the balance of power. What is needed, therefore, is a conception of justice which articulates the values and ideals of a democratic regime, 'specifying the aims the constitution is to achieve and the limits it must respect' (1987, 1). Only such a conception of justice has any hope of winning the support of an 'overlapping consensus' of opinion in a pluralist society.

This consideration also knocks out the second procedure political philosophy might follow, viz. one of constructing *comprehensive* conceptions of justice. For Rawls stability is gained by building an overlapping consensus of questions of political justice, so that the institutions of the basic structure may be justified to any and every citizen: 'justification in matters of political justice is addressed to others who disagree with us, and therefore . . . proceeds from some consensus' (1987, 6). Stability and social unity come from having a public standard which all can accept. But given the fact of pluralism, Rawls maintains, 'no general and comprehensive doctrine can assume the role of a publicly acceptable basis of political justice' (1987, 6). To defend this claim Rawls states 'a fifth general fact: we make many of our most important judgments subject to conditions which render it extremely unlikely that conscientious and fully reasonable persons, even after free discussion, can exercise their powers of reason so that all arrive at the same conclusion' (1989, 238).[4]

None of this is to suggest that Rawls thinks comprehensive doctrines unimportant. On the contrary, he argues that the citizens of a democratic society hold overall views which might be said to have two distinct parts. One part coincides with a political conception of justice, while the other forms a comprehensive doctrine 'to which the political conception is in some manner related' (1989, 249). For a society to be well-ordered (according to the precepts of justice as fairness) it is important that unreasonable comprehensive doctrines do not gain enough currency to undermine basic institutions of justice; but it is also necessary that citizens who hold to more reasonable comprehensive doctrines 'endorse justice as fairness as giving the content of their political judgments' (1989, 249). All individuals start from the standpoint of a comprehensive doctrine.

But to fulfil the tasks of political philosophy nothing is to be gained by developing a comprehensive philosophy, since our aim must be to find a 'workable' conception which will command allegiance. A philosophical conception which embraced controversial claims would not be likely to gain as many adherents as one which avoided doing so. For this reason, it is better that we go in search, not of answers to metaphysical or epistemological questions, but of 'practical' solutions to the problem of how to secure agreement. This is the aim of justice as fairness: 'it presents itself not as a conception of justice that is true, but one that can serve as a basis of informed and willing political agreement between citizens viewed as free and equal persons' (1985, 230). The objective, in the end, is not to be able to say to different groups of citizens, 'Here are the true principles of justice', but to be able to say, 'Here are principles we can all live with'. 'Philosophy as the search for truth about an independent metaphysical and moral order cannot . . . provide a workable and shared basis for a political conception of justice in a democratic society' (1985, 230).

From this conclusion it is clear that Rawls must now object to the liberalisms of Kant and Mill. They are both general and comprehensive moral doctrines:

> general in that they apply to a wide range of subjects, and comprehensive in that they include conceptions of what is of value in human life, ideals of personal virtue and character that are to inform our thought and conduct as a whole. Here we have in mind Kant's ideal of autonomy and his connecting it with the values of the Enlightenment, and Mill's ideal of individuality and his connecting it with the values of modernity. These two liberalisms both comprehend far more than the political. Their doctrines of free institutions rest in large part on ideals and values that are not generally, or perhaps even widely, shared in a democratic society. They are not a practical public basis of a political conception of justice, and I suspect the same is true of many liberalisms besides those of Kant and Mill. (1987, 6)

Thus it is that Rawls comes to abandon Kant – or at least the Kantian interpretation of his enterprise. If success in achieving consensus requires political philosophy to be 'independent and autonomous from other parts of philosophy, especially from philosophy's long-standing problems and controversies' (1987, 8), then the Kantian interpretation of justice as fairness is too controversial. And controversy must be avoided. Indeed, we must adopt the 'method of avoidance' so that 'differences between contending political views can at least be moderated', and 'social cooperation on the basis of mutual respect can be maintained' (1985, 231).

Now while Rawls abandons Kant, this does not mean that he abandons liberalism. He abandons the defence of liberalism as a comprehensive *moral* philosophy but he still promotes what he calls '*political* liberalism'. This is a liberalism which is not dependent upon any particular liberal moral ideal, such as autonomy. It remains a version of 'liberalism' inasmuch as it stresses the importance of toleration, and argues that the polity should be governed by principles which do not themselves presuppose that some particular form of the good life is best. Political liberalism's attitude to comprehensive liberal conceptions is therefore one of tolerance, since it looks to allow all competing moral ideals to compete in peace – as far as is practically possible.

Rawls's defence of this outlook is, in the end, a defence of a liberalism which will secure stability and social unity. This is the only standpoint that he thinks can secure it. In this respect, his political philosophy returns liberalism to one of its oldest concerns: peace. Indeed, we suggest that it gives Rawls's politics a decidedly Hobbesian flavour, since he now ties his conception of justice, not to autonomy or individuality, but *order*. (For an argument as to the Hobbesian nature of Rawls's view see Hampton 1989.)

What seems most problematic in all this is clearly Rawls's insistence on abandoning liberalism's reliance on comprehensive moral ideals. For it is not clear that Rawls is able to do so. He himself recognizes the difficulty, and takes it up in a discussion of the question of education. Some groups, such as various religious sects who oppose the culture of the modern world and wish to lead their common life apart from its foreign influences, may wish to bring up their children with these values. Should the state impose any educational requirements? The comprehensive liberalism of Kant would argue for the state to impose requirements designed to foster the values of autonomy. Political liberalism, however, requires much less. It will ask that children's education include such things as knowledge of their constitutional rights, so that they know that liberty of conscience exists and apostasy is not a legal crime. 'Moreover, their education should also prepare them to be fully cooperating members of society and enable them to be self-supporting; it should also encourage the political virtues so that they want to honour the fair terms of social cooperation in their relations with the rest of society' (1988, 267). Yet this does mean that the state, under the liberal political conception of justice as fairness, will require the inculcation of certain values which bear noteworthy resemblance to the values of the comprehensive liberalisms of Mill and Kant (1988, 268). The difficulty this poses is not fully answered by Rawls, who simply concedes that the 'unavoidable consequences of reasonable requirements for children's education may have to be accepted, often with regret' (1988, 268).

Nonetheless, Rawls's broaching of this question is revealing. First, it shows plainly that while his thought is moving away from the Kantian ideal which has dominated most of his work, the values of that comprehensive liberal conception still inform much of his thinking. Secondly, it suggests how much the motivation behind Rawls's revisions or re-interpretation of his theory of justice stem from an increasing concern with order or stability. There is a tension here between his inclination to say that education should promote certain liberal virtues, and his wish not to alienate those whose rejection of the liberal virtues threatens to undermine the basis of a stable social order. As his concern with order has grown, bringing with it a re-interpretation of his conception of justice as one which is best able to preserve a stable social unity, he has increasingly distanced himself from the Kantian ideal of freedom.

The point Rawls has now reached in the course of elaborating and defending his theory of justice is some distance away from his original conception. Not because the principles of justice themselves have changed dramatically; they haven't. What has shifted rather is the balance of justifications, and his understanding of the very point of engaging in the activity of political philosophy. So far we have tried simply to keep pace with these developments. But now it is time to take stock, and ask where the complications of this self-critique have led, and will lead in the future.

AN INTERPRETATION OF THE NEW RAWLS

Despite the changes in Rawls's thinking in the movements we have discussed, many continuities remain to link them with his early work. The two movements have turned out to be as much shifts of emphasis as anything else. But, as we noted at the outset, shifts of emphasis, when great enough, can amount to changes of substance. Differences of degree, when considerable, make for differences in kind. The argument we wish to put here is that certain shifts in emphasis have brought about an important qualitative change in the character of Rawls's political theory. And this change is not altogether welcome.

The shifts in emphasis come out most clearly in Rawls's increasing reliance on the *feasibility* arguments which dominated Part Three of his book, and in the corresponding down-playing of considerations of *desirability*. We agreed in chapter 4 that feasibility considerations are more important in *A Theory of Justice* than is generally recognized. In his later work they come to be more important still.

As we have seen, Rawls thinks that the important question is that of how to maintain an enduring social unity in a pluralist society like America. The task of political philosophy is not to find the answer to the question of what would be the most desirable principles of justice to govern a good society, but to develop 'workable' or feasible principles for this one. His own ambition is to construct a political conception of justice which is suitable 'for us'. Thus his ever greater emphasis on the need to find principles which can secure stability.

The stability Rawls is looking for, he insists time and again, is not the fleeting stability which comes with sound institutional design to moderate the contest for power among competing interests. Stability is a condition in which there is deep-seated agreement on fundamental questions about the basic structure of society. The ultimate requirement of feasibility of a conception of justice becomes a requirement that the conception be able to be used to order a society in which people differ greatly in their views of the good, and differ even in political philosophy. The focus on this requirement is what is perhaps most novel in the later work. In *A Theory of Justice* a conception is feasible just so long as it can meet the constraints of the concept of right: so long in particular as it can serve as a public means of resolving disputes. Now a feasible conception is required to be able to do this, even when the people involved hold to different moral philosophies.

The contractarian device of the original position is now re-interpreted by Rawls as a solution to the problem of finding a suitably feasible conception. It is a device used to model the reasoning of persons in modern society. The constraints on rational choice it imposes are taken to reflect the most important values and commitments to freedom and equality 'latent in the public political culture of a democratic society' (1988, 252). Under the reasonable conditions these constraints express, rational choice produces the principles of justice all can accept. Such principles amount to a conception of justice which is stable because they are principles which would be chosen by that society. These principles are therefore feasible.

Now this is not to suggest that Rawls has abandoned all interest in the question of what principles of justice are desirable. But that question is clearly of subordinate importance. All consideration of what principles are desirable is framed in the context of the question of what principles are most reasonable or feasible 'for us' (i.e., most likely to bring stability). In the OP this relationship between the feasible and the desirable is reflected in the relationship between the Reasonable and the Rational. The Reasonable (feasible) frames and subordinates the Rational (desirable). Indeed, for Rawls, it makes no sense to talk of what is rational in the abstract – although his critics still accuse him of doing so. We always start with the fundamental intuitive ideas of existing society.

Recognizing this points us to a surprising conclusion.

Despite the criticism he has always attracted from commentators like Sandel, who draw their ammunition from Hegel's arsenal, Rawls's developed theory turns out to have a decidedly Hegelian flavour. This is so, not because Rawls embraces Hegel's political philosophical conclusions, nor because he endorses Hegel's idealist metaphysics. It is because he takes as his starting point existing social practices – he does this in both the later stages of his thought, including the Kantian one – and looks to examine them in the light of the values embedded in them. Rawls does not intend simply to pluck his values out of the air. He looks to the actual social practices themselves, to the 'fundamental ideas viewed as latent in the public political culture of a democratic society' (1988, 252).

Why does this invite comparison with Hegel? To answer this we need to look briefly at some of Hegel's fundamental claims. Philosophers who abstract from actuality, Hegel believed, are usually led to build models out of thin air. Such models are not only of doubtful relevance but often dangerous (when their builders are tempted to use force to create their ideal city on earth). Philosophy, for Hegel, must deal with the actual world. This does not mean being content to describe appearances, or accepting the status quo. Rather it means taking the actual world as its object, and trying to understand the reason why it is as it is. It means bringing this reason into the open. It may even discover that 'the inner rationale of its [the actual world's] existence is totally different from what it appears to be to the uncritical mind, and it would then be the task of philosophy to reconcile appearance and content' (Avineri 1980, 125). Crucially, the philosopher must realize that the rationality of the actual world is a historical rationality; the world is not rational in any *abstract* sense. Kant's mistake was to try to evaluate the actual world by erecting an ideal kingdom which was 'transcendentally' rational – a world which existed not here but in the beyond, in the *noumenal* realm divorced from the world of reality. For Hegel, the ideal was to be found in the actual.

Rawls's view bears a striking resemblance to this account,

although he does not accept Hegel's metaphysical claims. Like Hegel, he insists that there is nothing to be gained by positing abstract principles or constructing noumenal realms. We begin our moral inquiries with existing societies. The OP is not the starting point in Rawls's philosophy but a way of modelling the values of an actual social order. The moral character of this actual order is expressed in Rawls's account of the intuitions latent in its *practices*. The Hegelian character of Rawls's philosophy lies in his understanding of his project not as a bid to re-model his society in the image of some rational ideal, but as an attempt to understand liberal democratic America by eliciting the principles latent in the (reasonable) intuitions of its public political culture.[5]

It must be admitted that this is not a conventional reading of Rawls. But there are several considerations which suggest that this interpretation of Rawls as he now understands his own philosophy is not only plausible but unsurprising. First, in his lectures on 'Kantian Constructivism in Moral Theory', Rawls paid tribute to John Dewey, the philosopher these lectures were to honour. Dewey's genius, he said, 'was to adapt much that is valuable in Hegel's idealism to a form of naturalism congenial to our culture' (1980, 516). One of Hegel's aims was to overcome the dualisms which he thought disfigured Kant's transcendental idealism, and Dewey shared this concern. 'In elaborating his moral theory along somewhat Hegelian lines, Dewey opposes Kant, sometimes quite explicitly, and often at the same places at which justice as fairness also departs from Kant.' 'Thus', Rawls concludes, 'there are a number of affinities between justice as fairness and Dewey's moral theory which are explained by the common aim of overcoming the dualisms in Kant's doctrines' (1980, 516). This common concern to overcome the flaws in Kant's moral theory would make it unsurprising if Rawls should, like Dewey, have come to develop a political philosophy which bears comparison with Hegel's.

Second, Rawls himself suggests, in 'The Idea of an Overlapping Consensus', that the conception of justification he has developed is at odds with the Hobbesian strand of liberal thought but 'plays a central role in Hegel's *Philosophy of Right*' (1987, 6n.).

Thirdly, and perhaps most importantly, Rawls sees himself as engaged in the task of finding a philosophical solution to a practical problem: the problem of bridging the impasse in recent American political history which reveals a lack of agreement on the way basic social institutions should be arranged if they are to conform to the freedom and equality of citizens as moral persons. To 'dispel the conflict between the different understandings of freedom and equality' (1980, 517) Rawls takes to be a practical as well as a philosophical task. The aim, remember, is to secure a stable social unity. But such a unity cannot be achieved by mere institutional (re-)design. Such an approach will not secure the allegiance to the institutions of the basic structure which is essential for stability. The only thing that will achieve this is a *public* philosophy governing the basic structure which all can live with, and use to justify to one another the basic institutions of society. *Philosophy* is crucial because it must be possible to articulate such a justification; otherwise there cannot be the requisite agreement – however long a peaceful *modus vivendi* is sustained – and there will be no stable social unity. Philosophy is needed to *conceive* how public agreement is possible. Rawls makes this clear in his defence of the 'method of avoidance' when he writes:

> this method may enable us to conceive how, given a desire for free and uncoerced agreement, a public understanding could arise consistent with the historical conditions and constraints of our social world. *Until we bring ourselves to conceive how this could happen, it can't happen*. (1985, 231 – emphasis added)

In giving this task to philosophy Rawls gives philosophy an importance also accorded it by Hegel who thought that in the reconciliation (Versöhnung) of the most important oppositions between man and nature, between man and society, and between man and God, philosophy played an indispensable role. These separations had brought with them certain benefits: 'Man only attains his self-conscious, rational autonomy in separating off from nature, society, God and fate' (Taylor 1979, 15). Philosophy had to show, not how to return to the primitive unity in which these oppositions were absent, but how these benefits can be retained in a world in which man is not alienated but at home. In his social philosophy, to the extent that it can be separated from his philosophy as a whole, Hegel wanted to show how man in the modern state could be free. Philosophy was crucial, moreover, inasmuch as its rational educative role is the key to community. As Raymond Plant explains, for Hegel,

> Modern man can live in an integrated political community so long as both his social and political and his religious experience is transfigured by philosophy. At the conventional level of thought man sees political institutions as imposed and arbitrary whereas the philosopher demonstrates that they are necessary in their development and expressive of the individual's will in character . . . only when such interpretations have been given can men live in community in the modern world. (Plant 1973, 182)

There is a sense in which Rawls is doing something very similar to Hegel. Political philosophy, in Rawls's account, tries to supply a solution to the problem of instability by identifying the deep bases of agreement in modern society. Once these are identified, they may be presented by members of society to each other in formulations which justify social arrangements and offer to the individual an assurance that he has a secure place in the world.

We have seen that, like Hegel, Rawls is opposed to the abstract philosophical approach to issues of justice. We have also noticed that he is against the purely practical approach that would cast such issues as matters of finding a satisfactory *modus vivendi* – and here too he resembles Hegel. But it must be said that in the second stage of his later development Rawls moves much nearer to a practical understanding of the theory of justice than any Hegelian could tolerate. In his most recent writings Rawls sees himself as going beyond the parochial debates between different political positions, for he now sees the task of political philosophy as practical rather than properly philosophical. It seeks a *practical* solution to a political problem rather than the truth about political morality. Pluralist societies, he argues, are ridden with disputes among competing moral, religious, and political ideas, so 'comprehensive' moral conceptions will only add to such conflict. We need, more than anything else, a *procedure* to adjudicate among these competing claims. Political philosophy's task is to devise this procedure.

It does this, in Rawls's account, by constructing principles of political justice. Yet these principles are established not by challenging and rejecting competing comprehensive conceptions but by trying, as far as is possible, to transcend and *accommodate* them. The point, after all, is not to find the truth about the principles of public morality, but to ensure social unity and stability in long-run equilibrium by forging a stable agreement among the various moral, religious and other comprehensive philosophies.

Here Rawls's philosophy looks to have most in common with the *pragmatism* of American thinkers like William James and John Dewey, rather than Hegel's political philosophy. Hegel insisted that the mediation of social conflict was a philosophical matter rather than one of 'practical' adjudication. Indeed he rejected the idea of making any distinction between philosophy, or theory, and practice in this regard. Rawls, in denying that the point of philosophical inquiry is to find the 'truth' about public morality and in emphasizing the need to secure practical, workable solutions to problems of fundamental social conflict, is closer to Dewey than to Hegel.[6]

With these most recent developments, we think, Rawls has taken an unfortunate turn. In regarding its task as that of forging a stable practical agreement among various comprehensive doctrines, Rawlsian philosophy can no longer see itself as just one among many competing political philosophies. Its aim, ultimately, is not to challenge or repudiate such competitors but to *subsume* them, by formulating a standpoint which will command their allegiance. Political philosophy, as Rawls conceives it, thus takes on a certain enabling role: it tries to articulate the terms of a political agreement which will allow a variety of standpoints to coexist in a stable social unity, thus ensuring that differing moral and political commitments are taken into consideration and accommodated rather than seen as positions on different sides of political debate. Yet, paradoxically, this conception of political philosophy, could it succeed, would eliminate political philosophy, for its primary concern is to end political argument by taking the most fundamental disputes 'off the political agenda' (1989, 253). For the sake of social stability it proposes to deal with the intractable moral and political disputes which characterize modern social life by instituting a practical agreement bringing the conversation about the most important matters to an end.

We think that Rawls is mistaken both in thinking that the conciliatory task can be fulfilled in the way he envisages and in identifying that task as the proper job of political philosophy. The conciliatory task is not likely to be fulfilled in the way he hopes for a number of reasons. First, the divisive questions that he would take off the political agenda are often those which people are most reluctant not to have addressed. Secondly, the tactic of seeking to take issues off the agenda does not always serve to conciliate; after all, it is distinctive of some of the least conciliatory comprehensive philosophies: consider Nozick's claim that the entitlements of individuals are not up for political negotiation. Finally, it remains to be established that an 'overlapping consensus' is necessary or sufficient for stability and social unity. (See Baier 1989)

Turning to our other reservation, we think that Rawls is also mistaken in identifying his conciliatory task as the proper job of political philosophy. If political philosophy occasionally serves to conciliate, it equally often serves to *give expression* to important conflicts within society about the ideals of social life. These conflicts are real and may be worth debating. By giving the conflicting ideals theoretical expression, political philosophies need not be concerned to transcend but rather to advance the debate among them. The point may be to bring conflict to the surface by formulating the claims of particular moral or political standpoints and thereby to facilitate conversation between those standpoints.

In serving such a function, it is quite legitimate for political philosophy to advance its claims by appealing to the truth of its conclusions; it may make claims about the right way to order social institutions – claims which it conceives to be epistemologically well grounded. It is a precondition of debate, properly understood, that the partners in that debate each view themselves at some level as having the weight of reason on their side; that is why each thinks there is some chance of persuading the other and some point therefore to the exchange. That each philosophy ascribes truth to its claims may simply reflect this assumption about the weight of reason.

Rawls, of course, has insisted that we should avoid making epistemological claims which draw on the assumptions of a comprehensive moral view. It is doubtful, however, whether even Rawls himself is able to obey these strictures. He concedes that 'whenever someone insists, for example, that certain questions are so fundamental that to ensure their being rightly settled justifies civil strife', we may have to assert 'certain aspects of our own comprehensive . . . doctrine' (1987, 14). But if he upholds the strictures, sticking to the latest view of his enterprise, then in effect what he is doing is despairing of reasoned debate on issues of conflicting political principle. He is announcing that the conversation is not worth the candle and that we should look for practical accommodation of different viewpoints, not intellectual exchange on fundamental issues. This note of despair is a far cry from the bravura of the earlier Rawls. We prefer the older, bolder tones.

SUMMARY

In his writings since the first publication of *A Theory of Justice*, Rawls has reinterpreted and further developed his political philosophy. We have tried to describe this development by tracing the shifts in his thinking. Two movements dominate his later thought: the first is an attempt to strengthen and refine the Kantian interpretation of his endeavours; the second is a distancing of his enterprise from Kant's comprehensive moral philosophy. In making the latter move, Rawls comes to place much greater emphasis on the need to secure practical agreement among competing religious and moral views, and to see this rather than the pursuit of truth as the task of political philosophy. We have treated this as an unwelcome development in Rawls's thought. It suggests an aspiration for the political philosophy to end all political philosophies. Yet it also suggests despair as to the possibility of anything being accomplished in politics by philosophical inquiry.

Notes

CHAPTER 1 A NEW DEPARTURE

1 Unless otherwise indicated, numbers in brackets refer to Rawls 1971, *A Theory of Justice*; where any name is necessary the abbreviation TJ is used. References to Rawls's other works are indicated only by date of publication and page number.

2 Although Rawls's main efforts in the study of what is feasible are directed to the problem of stability, we might note that his work has also generated other, more technical investigations of how far it measures up in feasibility terms. Thus one of the more interesting developments in the wake of *A Theory of Justice* was the proof that the two-principles proposal had attractive and indeed unusual social-theoretic properties. (See Hammond 1976, Strasnick 1976.)

3 For an excellent debate on the issue of moral individualism see the paper by Charles Taylor, and the replies by John Broome, Peter Gaerdenfors, Bob Goodin and Frank Jackson in Brennan and Walsh 1989.

CHAPTER 2 A CONTRACTARIAN THEORY

1 In describing Buchanan as a heuristic contractarian, we are assuming that he should be read so that choice is indicative of preference, not constitutive of it. If choice is constitutive of preference, as in revealed preference theory, then Buchanan would count as a definitional contractarian. Unanimous agree-

ment would be definitional of Pareto-optimality, not merely indicative of it.

2 Scanlon offers an interesting recasting of Rawls, 123 and following.

CHAPTER 5 THE LIBERTARIAN CRITIQUE

1 Many libertarians write sometimes in a pragmatic vein, sometimes in a principled. See for example Hospers 1971.

CHAPTER 7 THE SELF-CRITIQUE

1 A succinct analysis of the shifts in Rawls's thinking has been presented by Richard Arneson (1989, 696–9). He identifies three significant changes in Rawls's theory since *A Theory of Justice* was first published. The first change involved a revision of the account of the OP which emphasizes the priority given by the parties therein to their Kantian interests in developing and exercising their moral powers of rational autonomy and fair dealing. Principles chosen in the OP are then justified by appealing to this ideal of the person – an ideal Rawls now holds to be consistent with the self-understanding of the ordinary citizen in a democratic culture. The second alleged change follows from this insofar as Rawls now no longer sees himself as engaged in a search for universal principles of justice: the validity of his ideal, he maintains, is relative to modern democratic society. The third change in Rawls's thinking, Arneson argues, is in his emphasis that 'justice as fairness' is a *political* conception of justice rather than a comprehensive moral conception. As such, its concern is to secure an 'overlapping consensus' in a pluralistic society so as to produce social unity despite deep disagreements among citizens. Our own, more detailed, account of the development of Rawls's theory of justice is quite consistent with that offered by Arneson. However, we tend to see the first two changes Arneson discusses as aspects of the same movement toward a strengthened form of Kantianism. The third change we interpret as symptomatic of Rawls's later rejection of Kantianism.

2 Here we should note that Rawls now says that what is to count as a primary good is determined not by any empirical or

historical survey of what human beings need, but by the conception of moral persons as having certain highest-order interests. In other words, the notion of primary goods provides an account of what moral persons in a well-ordered society would prefer. This account offers no psychological or sociological theses about what people want, but ties primary goods to the conception of the person implicit in liberal democratic America. In this Rawls makes a very clear revision of the account in *A Theory of Justice*.

3 On liberty and liberties see Pettit 1989b.

4 Rawls provides an important discussion of the sources or causes of disagreement between reasonable persons in his account of the 'burdens of reason' in 'The Domain of the Political and Overlapping Consensus' (1989, 235–8).

5 There is an intriguing parallel between Rawls's account of the relationship between the Reasonable and the Rational and Hegel's view of the relationship between the 'actual' and the 'rational'. In a famous passage Hegel stated that 'What is rational is actual and what is actual is rational' (Hegel 1978, 10). By this he did not mean that everything that exists is rational. Rather, he suggests that while rationality is presupposed by actuality, rationality can only manifest itself in the actual world. Like Hegel, Rawls thinks that the actual or Reasonable presupposes the Rational: social cooperation makes no sense unless we assume persons to be rational and capable of having conceptions of the good. But again, the rational makes no sense on its own; mere rationality cannot legislate for us. Only when it is constrained by the Reasonable can it give us conclusions of substance; just as for Hegel *a priori* rationality will give us only abstractions. The limitations of this comparison lie in the differences between the understandings of rationality in Hegel and Rawls. For Hegel the rational is associated with the working out of God's purposes in the actual world; it is not clear that his notion of rationality can sensibly be shorn of these metaphysical claims. Rawls's idea of rationality is considerably more austere.

6 Dewey, of course, was greatly influenced by Hegel, as Rawls himself recognizes (Rawls 1980). Among modern philosophers, Rawls would probably receive a most sympathetic hearing from the American pragmatist, Richard Rorty (see Rorty 1982, especially Introduction and chapter 9).

Bibliography

Arneson, Richard 1989, 'Introduction' (to a Symposium on Rawlsian Theory of Justice: Recent Developments), *Ethics*, 99, 695–710.

Arrow, K. J. 1951, *Social Choice and Individual Values*, New Haven: Yale University Press, (2nd edn 1963).

Avineri, S. 1980, *Hegel's Theory of the Modern State*, Cambridge: Cambridge University Press.

Baier, Kurt 1989, 'Justice and the Aims of Political Philosophy', *Ethics*, 99, 771–90.

Barry, Brian 1965, *Political Argument*, London: Routledge & Kegan Paul.

Barry, Brian 1973, *The Liberal Theory of Justice*, Oxford: Oxford University Press.

Barry, Brian 1989, *A Treatise on Social Justice. Volume 1: Theories of Justice*, London: Harvester-Wheatsheaf.

Benn, Stanley and Peters, Richard 1959, *Social Principles and the Democratic State*, London: Allen and Unwin.

Berlin, Isaiah 1969, *Four Essays on Liberty*, Oxford: Oxford University Press.

Bonner, John 1986, *Politics, Economics and Welfare*, Brighton: Wheatsheaf Books.

Brennan, Geoffrey 1987, 'The Buchanan Contribution', *Finanzarchiv*, Band 45, 1–24.

Brennan, Geoffrey and Walsh, Cliff (eds) 1989, *Rathionality, Individualism and Public Policy*, Canberra: Centre for Federal Financial Relations, Australian National University.

Broome, John 1989, 'Comments on "Irreducibly Social Goods" by Charles Taylor', in Brennan and Walsh, 1989.

Buchanan, Allen E. 1989, 'Assessing the Communitarian Critique of Liberalism', *Ethics*, 99, 852–82.

Buchanan, J. M. and Tullock, G. 1962, *The Calculus of Consent*, Ann Arbor: University of Michigan Press.

Daniels, N. 1978, *Reading Rawls: Critical Studies of* A Theory of Justice, Oxford: Basil Blackwell.

Doppelt, Gerald 1989, 'Is Rawls's Kantian Liberalism Coherent and Defensible?', *Ethics*, 99, 815–51.

Dworkin, R. M. 1978, 'Liberalism', in S. Hampshire (ed.), *Public and Private Morality*, Cambridge: Cambridge University Press, 113–43.

Elster, Jon 1986, 'The Market and the Forum: Three Varieties of Political Theory', in J. Elster and A. Hylland (eds), *Foundations of Social Choice Theory*, Cambridge: Cambridge University Press.

Fishkin, James and Laslett, Peter 1979, *Philosophy, Politics and Society*, 5th Series, Oxford: Basil Blackwell.

Fisk, Milton 1978, 'History and Reason in Rawls' Moral Theory', in N. Daniels (ed.), *Reading Rawls. Critical Studies of* A Theory of Justice, Oxford: Basil Blackwell, 53–80.

Galston, William A. 1989, 'Pluralism and Social Unity', *Ethics*, 99, 711–26.

Gaus, G. F. 1983, *The Modern Liberal Theory of Man*, New York: St. Martin's Press.

Gauthier, David 1986, *Morals By Agreement*, Oxford: Oxford University Press.

Gutmann, Amy 1985, 'Communitarian Critics of Liberalism', *Philosophy and Public Affairs*, 14, 308–22.

Habermas, Jürgen 1973, 'Wahrheitstheoriem', in *Wirklichkeit und Reflexion: Walter Schulz zum 60 Geburtstag*, Pfullingen: Neske.

Hamlin, Alan 1989, 'Liberty, Contract, and the State', in Hamlin and Pettit (eds), *The Good Polity*, Oxford: Basil Blackwell.

Hamlin, Alan and Pettit, Philip 1989, 'The Normative Analysis of the State; Some Preliminaries' in Hamlin and Pettit (eds), *The Good Polity*, Oxford: Basil Blackwell.

Hammond, P. J. 1976, 'Equity, Arrow's Conditions & Rawls's "Difference Principle"', *Econometrica*, 44, 793–800.

Hampton, Jean 1989, 'Should Political Philosophy Be Done without Metaphysics?', *Ethics*, 99, 791–814.

Hare, R. M. 1978, 'Rawls's Theory of Justice', in N. Daniels (ed.),

Reading Rawls. Critical Studies of A Theory of Justice, Oxford: Basil Blackwell, 81–107.

Harsanyi, John 1976, *Essays on Ethics, Social Behaviour and Scientific Explanation*, Dordrecht: Reidel.

Hart, H. L. A. 1978, 'Rawls on Liberty and Its Priority', in N. Daniels (ed.), *Reading Rawls. Critical Studies of* A Theory of Justice, Oxford: Basil Blackwell, 230–53.

Hayek, F. A. 1960, *The Constitution of Liberty*, London: Routledge & Kegan Paul.

Hegel, G. 1978, *The Philosophy of Right*, trans. T. M. Knox, Oxford: Oxford University Press.

Hospers, John 1971, *Libertarianism*, Los Angeles: Nash.

Jackson, Michael W. 1986, *Matters of Justice*, London: Croom Helm.

Kukathas, Chandran 1989a, *Hayek and Modern Liberalism*, Oxford: Oxford University Press.

Kukathas, Chandran 1989b, 'Welfare, Contract, and the Language of Charity', *Philosophical Quarterly*, 39, 75–80.

Kymlicka, Will 1988, 'Liberalism and Communitarianism', *Canadian Journal of Philosophy*, 18, 181–204.

Kymlicka, Will 1989, 'Liberal Individualism and Liberal Neutrality', *Ethics*, 99, 883–905.

Larmore, Charles 1987, *Patterns of Moral Complexity*, Cambridge: Cambridge University Press.

Lukes, Steven 1973, *Individualism*, Oxford: Basil Blackwell.

Lukes, Steven 1978, 'No Archimedean Point', in his *Essays in Social Theory*, London: Macmillan, 187–90.

MacIntyre, Alasdair 1986, *After Virtue. A Study in Moral Theory*, 2nd edn, London: Duckworth.

McLean, Iain 1987, *Public Choice*, Oxford: Basil Blackwell.

Miller, David 1976, *Social Justice*, Oxford: Oxford University Press.

Nozick, Robert 1974, *Anarchy, State and Utopia*, New York: Basic Books.

Pettit, Philip 1974, 'A Theory of Justice?', *Theory and Decision*, 4, 311–24.

Pettit, Philip 1980, *Judging Justice: An Introduction to Contemporary Political Philosophy*, London: Routledge and Kegan Paul.

Pettit, Philip 1982, 'Habermas on Truth and Justice', in G. H. R. Parkinson (ed.), *Marx and Marxisms*, Cambridge: Cambridge University Press.

Pettit, Philip 1986, 'Free Riding and Foul Dealing', *Journal of y*, 83, 361–79; reprinted in the *Philosopher's Annual*,

ilip 1987, 'Rights, Constraints and Trumps', *Analysis*, 47,

, Philip 1988a, 'The Consequentialist Can Recognise Rights', *hilosophical Quarterly*, 35, 537–51.

Pettit, Philip 1988b, 'The Defence of Liberalism', in Knud Haakonssen (ed.), *Traditions of Liberalism*, Sydney: Centre for Independent Studies.

Pettit, Philip 1989a, 'The Freedom of the City: A Republican Ideal', in Alan Hamlin and Philip Pettit (eds), *The Good Polity*, Oxford: Basil Blackwell.

Pettit, Philip 1989b, 'A Definition of Negative Liberty', *Ratio*, 2.

Pettit, Philip 1990, 'Consequentialism', in Peter Singer (ed.), *A Companion to Ethics*, Oxford: Basil Blackwell.

Pettit, Philip *The Common Mind: From Folk Psychology to Social and Political Theory*, Oxford: Oxford University Press (forthcoming).

Plamenatz, John 1960, 'The Use of Political Theory'. *Political Studies*, 8, 37–47.

Plant, Raymond 1973, *Hegel*, London: Allen and Unwin.

Pogge, T. W. 1989, *Realizing Rawls*, Ithaca: Cornell University Press.

Rawls, John 1951, 'Outline of a Decision Procedure for Ethics', *Philosophical Review*, 60, 177–97.

Rawls, John 1957, 'Justice as Fairness', *Journal of Philosophy*, 54, 653–62.

Rawls, John 1971, *A Theory of Justice*, Oxford: Oxford University Press.

Rawls, John 1974, 'Concepts of Distributional Equity. Some Reasons for the Maximin Criterion', *American Economic Review*, 64, 141–6.

Rawls, John 1974–5, 'The Independence of Moral Theory', *Proceedings and Addresses of The American Philosophical Association*, 47.

Rawls, John 1975, 'Fairness to Goodness', *Philosophical Review*, 84, 536–54.

Rawls, John 1978, 'The Basic Structure as Subject', in A. Goldman and J. Kim (eds), *Values and Morals*, Boston: Reidel, 47–71 (an earlier version was first published in *American*

Philosophical Quarterly, 1977, Vol. 14, 159–65).

Rawls, John 1979, 'A Well-ordered Society', in P. Laslett and J. Fishkin (eds), *Philosophy, Politics and Society*, 5th series, 6–20.

Rawls, John 1980, 'Kantian Constructivism in Moral Theory', *The Journal of Philosophy*, 88, 515–72.

Rawls, John 1982a, 'The Basic Liberties and Their Priority', in S. MacMurrin (ed.), *The Tanner Lectures on Human Values*, Cambridge: Cambridge University Press, iii, 1–89.

Rawls, John 1982b, 'Social Unity and Primary Goods', in A. Sen and B. Williams (eds), *Utilitarianism and Beyond*, Cambridge: Cambridge University Press, 159–85.

Rawls, John 1985, 'Justice as Fairness: Political not Metaphysical', *Philosophy and Public Affairs*, 14, 223–51.

Rawls, John 1987, 'The Idea of an Overlapping Consensus', *Oxford Journal of Legal Studies*, 7, 1–25.

Rawls, John 1988, 'The Priority of Right and Ideas of the Good', *Philosophy and Public Affairs*, 17, 251–76.

Rawls, John 1989, 'The Domain of the Political and Overlapping Consensus', *New York University Law Review*, 64, 233–55.

Raz, Joseph 1979, 'The Rule of Law and its Virtue', in Raz, *The Authority of Law*, Oxford: Oxford University Press, 210–29.

Raz, Joseph 1986, *The Morality of Freedom*, Oxford: Oxford University Press.

Rorty, Richard 1982, *Consequences of Pragmatism (Essays: 1972–1980)*, Brighton: Harvester Press.

Sandel, Michael 1982, *Liberalism and the Limits of Justice*, Cambridge: Cambridge University Press.

Sandel, Michael 1988, 'The Political Theory of the Procedural Republic', *Revue de Metaphysique et de Morale*, 93, 57–68.

Scanlon, T. M. 1982, 'Contractualism and Utilitarianism', in A. Sen and B. Williams (eds), *Utilitarianism and Beyond*, Cambridge: Cambridge University Press.

Seidman, S. 1983, *Liberalism and the Origins of European Social Theory*, Oxford: Basil Blackwell.

Sen, Amartya 1970, *Collective Choice and Social Welfare*, San Francisco: Holden-Day.

Steiner, H. 1978, 'Can a Social Contract Be Signed By An Invisible Hand?', in G. Parry, N. Birnbaum and J. Lively (eds), *Democracy, Consensus and Social Contract*, London: Sage, 295–316.

Strasnick, S. 1976, 'Social Choice Theory and the Derivation of Rawls "Difference Principle"', *Journal of Philosophy*, 73, 85–99.

Taylor, Charles 1979, *Hegel and Modern Society*, Cambridge: Cambridge University Press.

Taylor, Charles 1985, 'Atomism', in his *Philosophical Papers*, 2 vols, Cambridge: Cambridge University Press, ii, 187–210.

Walzer, Michael 1981, 'Philosophy and Democracy', *Political Theory*, 9, 379–99.

Walzer, Michael 1983, *Spheres of Justice*, Oxford: Basil Blackwell.

Wolff, R. P. 1977, *Understanding Rawls. A Reconstruction and Critique of* A Theory of Justice, Princeton: Princeton University Press.

Index